LOSING THE PROMISED LAND

Elisha and the Kings of Judah

JOHN MACARTHUR

THOMAS NELSON
Since 1798

NASHVILLE   DALLAS   MEXICO CITY   RIO DE JANEIRO

Published in Nashville, Tennessee, by Thomas Nelson. Thomas Nelson is a registered trademark of Thomas Nelson, Inc.

Published in association with the literary agency of Wolgemuth & Associates, Inc.

Layout, design, and writing assistance by Gregory C. Benoit Publishing, Old Mystic, CT. GCB

Thomas Nelson, Inc. titles may be purchased in bulk for educational, business, fund-raising, or sales promotional use. For information, please e-mail *SpecialMarkets@ThomasNelson.com* .

ISBN 978-1-4185-3692-3

Printed in the United States of America

09 10 11 12 13 WC 5 4 3 2 1

CONTENTS

⁓ ᵔ ⁓

THE DIVIDED KINGDOM

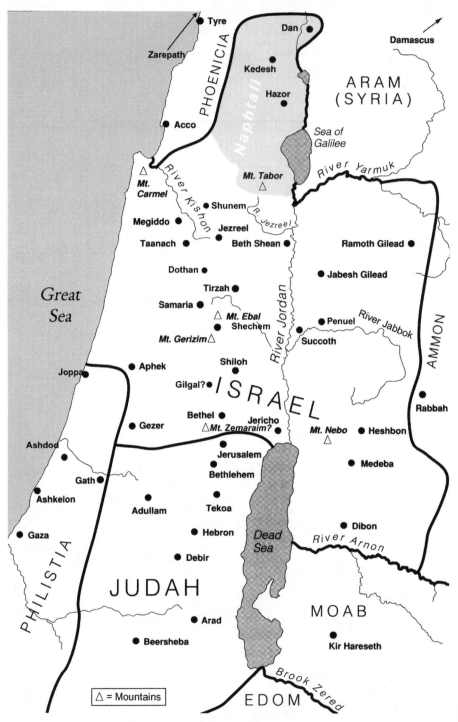

Tyre

Zarepath

PHOENICIA

Dan

Damascus

Kedesh

Hazor

ARAM
(SYRIA)

Naphtali

Acco

Sea of
Galilee

River Kishon

River Yarmuk

Mt.
Carmel

Mt. Tabor

Shunem

Megiddo

Jezreel

R. Jezreel

Taanach

Beth Shean

Ramoth Gilead

Great
Sea

Dothan

Jabesh Gilead

Tirzah

Samaria

River Jabbok

Mt. Ebal
Shechem

Penuel

AMMON

Mt. Gerizim

Succoth

River Jordan

Joppa

Aphek

Shiloh

Gilgal?

ISRAEL

Rabbah

Bethel

Jericho

Gezer

Mt. Zemaraim?

Mt. Nebo

Heshbon

Ashdod

Jerusalem

Gath

Bethlehem

Medeba

Ashkelon

Adullam

Tekoa

Gaza

Dibon

Hebron

Dead
Sea

River Arnon

Debir

JUDAH

MOAB

Arad

Beersheba

Kir Hareseth

△ = Mountains

Brook Zered

EDOM

INTRODUCTION

The nation of Israel began as one unified state, composed of twelve tribes of God's chosen people and living in the promised land. Under King David, the nation had vanquished its enemies and found the blessing that God had promised them. But all that changed when David's son Solomon added pagan elements to the proper worship of the Lord and led Israel away from God's Word. God responded to this sin by dividing the nation in two; He left ten tribes in the north, who retained the name Israel, and He left two in the south—the tribes of Judah and Benjamin—who called themselves Judah.

While Israel experienced a long line of terrible kings, each one seemingly more sinful than his predecessor, Judah retained the line of David. Certainly she also experienced evil kings, but there were a number who followed in David's footsteps by striving to keep the Lord's commands. In the midst of these tumultuous times, God consistently sent prophets to both Israel and Judah, pleading with His people to turn away from sin—but in the end, Judah went into captivity, just as Israel had more than a hundred years earlier.

In these twelve studies, we will jump back and forth in chronological history, looking at one historical period and then skipping forward or backward in time as needed. We will examine the lives of various kings, both good and bad, and we will also get to know a number of other interesting individuals. As we do, we will learn what it means to serve God with a whole heart, and we will see the supreme importance of preserving His Word in our homes and churches. Through it all, we will discover some precious truths about the character of God, and we will observe His great faithfulness in keeping His promises. We will learn, in short, what it means to walk by faith.

ᐁ WHAT WE'LL BE STUDYING ᐃ

This study guide is divided into four distinct sections in which we will examine selected Bible passages:

SECTION 1: HISTORY. In this first section, we will focus on the historical setting of our Bible text. These five lessons will give a broad overview of the people, places, and events that are important to this study. They will also provide the background for the next two sections. This is our most purely historical segment, focusing simply on what happened and why.

SECTION 2: CHARACTERS. The four lessons in this section will give us an opportunity to zoom in on the characters from our Scripture passages. Some of these people were introduced in section 1, but in this part of the study guide we will take a much closer look at these personalities. Why did God see fit to include them in His Book in the first place? What made them unique? What can we learn from their lives? In this practical section, we will answer all of these questions and more, as we learn how to live wisely by emulating the wisdom of those who came before us.

SECTION 3: THEMES. Section 3 consists of two lessons in which we will consider some of the broader themes and doctrines touched on in our selected Scripture passages. This is the guide's most abstract portion, wherein we will ponder specific doctrinal and theological questions that are important to the church today. As we ask what these truths mean to us as Christians, we will also look for practical ways to base our lives upon God's truth.

SECTION 4: SUMMARY AND REVIEW. In our final section, we will look back at the principles that we have discovered in the scriptures throughout this study guide. These will be our "takeaway" principles, those which permeate the Bible passages that we have studied. As always, we will be looking for ways to make these truths a part of our everyday lives.

⌁ ABOUT THE LESSONS ⌁

⌁ Each study begins with an introduction that provides the background for the selected Scripture passages.

⌁ To assist you in your reading, a section of notes—a miniature Bible commentary of sorts—offers both cultural information and additional insights.

⌁ A series of questions is provided to help you dig a bit deeper into the Bible text.

⌁ Overriding principles brought to light by the Bible text will be studied in each lesson. These principles summarize a variety of doctrines and practical truths found throughout the Bible.

⌁ Finally, additional questions will help you mine the deep riches of God's Word and, most importantly, to apply those truths to your own life.

SECTION 1:

HISTORY

In This Section:

THE FIRST KINGS OF JUDAH

1 KINGS 14–15; 2 CHRONICLES 13

✍ HISTORICAL BACKGROUND ✍

When the Lord brought the Israelites out of Egypt, He led them into the promised land of Canaan. There they were commanded to drive out the Canaanites so their evil paganism and false religions would not have a foothold in the land. Unfortunately, the Israelites failed to expel the Canaanites, and this failure brought them much sin and sorrow. But eventually the Lord raised up a king: David, a man after God's own heart, a ruler who led by example and followed God's Word with his whole heart.

Sadly, David's son Solomon did not follow in his father's footsteps. His reign started strong, as he initially desired to serve the Lord with wisdom and faithfulness. But as time went along, Solomon married numerous wives, many of whom were non-Israelites, in direct contradiction to the Lord's command to not marry foreigners (Deuteronomy 7:1–3; 17:17). This led Solomon to set up pagan shrines and to imitate the Canaanite "high places," sites of worship to false gods, which the Lord had commanded His people to destroy.

As a result of Solomon's disobedience, the Lord split the kingdom of Israel into two separate nations: the Northern Kingdom of Israel, and the Southern Kingdom of Judah. In this study, we will meet the first two kings of Judah: Rehoboam and Abijam (also spelled Abijah).

✍ READING 1 KINGS 14:21–28 ✍

JUDAH UNDER REHOBOAM: *Rehoboam, Solomon's son, takes the throne in Judah, leading the people into idolatry.*

21. REHOBOAM: Solomon's son. King Solomon had drifted away from obedience to God's Word, and the Lord had told him that He would tear the kingdom of Israel from his descendants—but He would leave one tribe under the authority of his son, the tribe of Judah. See the previous book in this series, *A House Divided*, for further background.

THE CITY WHICH THE LORD HAD CHOSEN: The Lord had commanded His people to worship Him at the city that He would set apart, which was Jerusalem (Deuteronomy 12:1–14; 1 Kings 9:3). Jeroboam, Israel's first king after the nation was divided, had set up idols in various places around the northern tribes, creating new worship centers for the people of Israel—effectively replacing Jerusalem as the center of worship and luring the Israelites to idolatry.

NAAMAH, AN AMMONITESS: Solomon's heart was led astray from following the Lord through his many marriages to pagan women. It is entirely possible that Naamah had led Solomon into the paganism of her Ammonite heritage (1 Kings 11:5). Whether or not she was influential in Solomon's idolatry, she undoubtedly had that effect on her son Rehoboam.

23. HIGH PLACES, SACRED PILLARS, AND WOODEN IMAGES: These were all associated with pagan idolatry. The high places were heathen worship sites that had been used by the Canaanites prior to Israel's arrival in the promised land. The sacred pillars were stones that had been set up vertically and dedicated to some pagan deity, sometimes with the god's name inscribed. The wooden images were probably Asherah poles, symbols of the goddess Asherah and associated with the licentious practices of Canaanite nature religions. The Lord had expressly commanded His people to destroy all these elements of paganism when they arrived in Canaan (Deuteronomy 12:2–4).

ON EVERY HIGH HILL AND UNDER EVERY GREEN TREE: This phrase is a quotation from Deuteronomy 12:2. The author of 1 Kings may have been intentionally drawing his readers' attention to the fact that the worship practices of Israel and Judah were in direct contradiction to God's Word.

24. PERVERTED PERSONS: These were male prostitutes who practiced wickedness at the pagan shrines in Canaan. Sexual license was an integral part of Canaanite nature religions, which taught that such practices would ensure a good harvest.

ALL THE ABOMINATIONS OF THE NATIONS: The author underscored the fact that the Lord had cast out the Canaanites and given the land to the descendants of Israel for the very fact that they had engaged in such wicked practices (Deuteronomy 18:9–12)—yet now the people of Israel had adopted those practices themselves. This was a dire warning of God's coming judgment, when He would also drive the children of Israel out of the promised land because of these sins. The fact that Israel was God's chosen nation did not give them license to engage in such iniquity; on the contrary, the Lord held them to a higher standard *because* they were His chosen people. If He had driven out the Canaanites for such sins, He would also drive out Israel.

27. KING REHOBOAM MADE BRONZE SHIELDS IN THEIR PLACE: These were ceremonial shields, used as part of the "dress uniform" of the palace guards. Shields used in battle were generally reinforced with iron, which is much harder than bronze but not as attractive. The decline from gold to bronze is quite telling regarding Judah's spiritual condition: bronze shines like gold, but it is only a cheap imitation.

⤳ READING 1 KINGS 15:1–8 ⤵

ABIJAM TAKES THE THRONE: *Rehoboam's son Abijam takes the throne after his father's death, and continues his father's idolatry.*

1. **ABIJAM:** Rehoboam's son, also spelled Abijah.

2. **MAACHAH THE GRANDDAUGHTER OF ABISHALOM:** Abishalom may refer to Absalom, King David's son. Abijam, therefore, would be David's great-great-grandson.

3. **THE HEART OF HIS FATHER DAVID:** David was a man after God's own heart (1 Samuel 13:14), meaning he strove all his life to walk in obedience to God's Word. Rehoboam, by contrast, had walked according to the desires of the flesh, leading him to do great wickedness. The kings of Judah are generally categorized as either walking as David had walked, or walking in the sins of their fathers.

4. **FOR DAVID'S SAKE:** The Lord had promised King David that his heirs would always occupy the throne in Jerusalem (2 Samuel 7:12–16). This promise was ultimately fulfilled in the person of Christ, whose kingdom is established forever.

5. **DAVID DID WHAT WAS RIGHT IN THE EYES OF THE LORD:** David's life was characterized by obedience to God's commands and by a desire to walk faithfully with the Lord. The "matter of Uriah the Hittite" refers to David's adultery with Bathsheba and murder of her husband, Uriah. This grievous sin brought lasting consequences to David's whole family, yet even at that time David demonstrated his desire to serve God by repenting when confronted by the prophet Nathan. For further study on David's life, see book 7 in this series, *Restoration of a Sinner*.

6. **THERE WAS WAR BETWEEN REHOBOAM AND JEROBOAM:** That is, between the house of Rehoboam and Jeroboam. Abijam's father, Rehoboam, was dead by this time.

⤳ READING 2 CHRONICLES 13:1–21 ⤵

ANOTHER SIDE OF ABIJAM: *The author of Chronicles sheds some additional light on the life of Abijam, showing that he was not entirely given over to evil.*

1. ABIJAH: This is the same man as Abijam in 1 Kings.

3. FOUR HUNDRED THOUSAND . . . EIGHT HUNDRED THOUSAND: This was no small skirmish, but open war between Judah and Israel. In this we see the severe repercussions of sin in the descendants of Jacob: the nation had been divided into two separate kingdoms, and now God's chosen people were trying to destroy one another.

4. MOUNT ZEMARAIM: The exact location is uncertain, but this was probably just north of the boundary between Israel and Judah, near Bethel. See the map in the Introduction.

6. JEROBOAM . . . ROSE UP AND REBELLED AGAINST HIS LORD: The Lord had actually ordained that Jeroboam should become king over Israel after the death of Solomon, in response to Solomon's lack of faithfulness to God's Word. See 1 Kings 11:26–40.

7. REHOBOAM WAS YOUNG AND INEXPERIENCED: The people of Israel had asked Rehoboam to alleviate their tax burden, and he responded by threatening to increase their load instead, thereby alienating the nation. Rehoboam was actually forty-one years old at the time of the division, and his foolishness was the immediate cause of the division of the kingdom. (See 1 Kings 12 for the entire account.)

8. THE GOLD CALVES WHICH JEROBOAM MADE: Jeroboam, the first king of the ten northern tribes, had created golden calves for the people to worship, leading Israel away from obedience to God's Word. The idea of representing Yahweh in the form of a calf came from Aaron in the wilderness (Exodus 32:1–4).

9. CAST OUT THE PRIESTS OF THE LORD: Jeroboam had replaced God's ordained priesthood, the sons of Aaron, with anyone he chose. He also told the people of Israel that they were free to worship God at various centers that he had appointed, each with its own golden calf, rather than make the journey to Jerusalem as the Lord had commanded.

11. YOU HAVE FORSAKEN HIM: Abijah's assessment was accurate at this point: to create one's own form of religion is to forsake the Lord. Those who want to walk faithfully with the Lord will obey His commands fully, avoiding the temptation to ignore some parts of His Word or to add their own rules and regulations.

CIVIL WAR: *The army of Israel disregards Abijam's counsel. The army of Judah calls upon the Lord, and He gives them a victory.*

14. THEY CRIED OUT TO THE LORD: The army of Israel was expecting some golden idols to give them victory, while Judah's army cried out to the Lord for protection. The results speak for themselves: the Lord is always faithful to guide and protect those who call out to Him.

17. FIVE HUNDRED THOUSAND CHOICE MEN OF ISRAEL FELL SLAIN: This was both a victory and a great tragedy. The Lord had shown Himself faithful to Judah when they cried out to Him, and He had demonstrated conclusively that He alone can give victory. Yet His chosen nation was divided against itself, and brother was taking up arms against brother—and this was not His desire for Israel.

21. ABIJAH GREW MIGHTY: The author of 2 Chronicles refrained from making a statement concerning Abijah's spiritual condition, contrary to the author of 1 Kings. Abijah's reign was characterized by some good and some wickedness. Like Solomon before him, he did not serve the Lord wholeheartedly; "his heart was not loyal to the LORD his God, as was the heart of his father David" (1 Kings 11:4).

⮑ FIRST IMPRESSIONS ⮐

1. *Why did God want the people of Israel to drive out the Canaanites? Why did He not just have them coexist peacefully?*

2. *Why did God command the Israelites to destroy the high places and sacred pillars when they arrived in Canaan? Why did the Israelites not obey?*

3. What led the nation of Judah into idolatry? What led the nation of Israel into idolatry?

4. What led Israel to divide into two separate nations? What resulted from this division? How could it have been avoided?

⌁ Some Key Principles ⌁

The Lord always keeps His promises.

The Lord promised David that his descendants would sit on the throne in Jerusalem and that his throne would be established forever. Further, the Lord assured David that He would be a father to Solomon, promising also to "chasten him with the rod of men" (2 Samuel 7:14) if Solomon should fall into sin. Solomon did eventually turn away from God, and the Lord kept His promise, disciplining Solomon by tearing away most of the kingdom from Solomon's own son Rehoboam. Yet at the same time, the Lord kept His promise to David by allowing Judah to retain the line of David.

Similarly, the Lord swore to Jeroboam that his descendants would always sit on the throne of Israel, provided that Jeroboam, like David, would obey God's commands and walk faithfully according to His Word (1 Kings 11:38). The implication of this promise, however, was that the Lord would not establish Jeroboam's throne if he did *not* walk in faithfulness—and that, unfortunately, is just how it turned out. Jeroboam led the northern tribes into idolatry, and the Lord removed him from the throne, just as He promised He would.

In keeping His promises to David and Jeroboam, the Lord established the Messianic line in Judah. Jeroboam's idolatry made it clear that true Messianic hope could only be found in a descendent of David, and as long as Judah existed, there was a descendent of David as her king. Even though Judah was eventually removed from the land, God's promise to David was eventually realized in Jesus, a descendant of David, who reigns in heaven over His people now and forevermore.

The world's idols cannot save.

Israel's king Jeroboam had established golden calves that were to be the new focus of the Israelites' worship. His intention was to draw the people of Israel away from worshiping at the temple in Jerusalem. In doing so, Jeroboam was attempting to solidify the split between the twelve tribes. But Jeroboam's plan had larger ramifications than that; some years later, Israel's army carried those same golden calves into battle, placing their entire faith in man-made idols for victory in combat.

Abijah, by contrast, openly declared, "God Himself is with us as our head" (2 Chronicles 13:12), and Judah's army placed their trust in the Lord. That trust was not misplaced; neither was their faith a form of weakness or cowardice—quite the reverse. The Lord quickly vindicated the army of Judah by miraculously intervening on their behalf, and they routed the army of Israel. Indeed, the entire conflict might have been avoided if Israel had turned away from their golden calves and heeded the sound advice that Abijah offered.

The world today still urges us to place our faith in false idols, such as wealth, prestige, or self-reliance, yet these things are no more effective than a statue of a cow. The devil does not care what we place our faith in, as long as it is not the God who created us. But the fact is idols are powerless to rescue people from their troubles.

The Lord is in control, even when His people are foolish.

Even during Solomon's life the Lord had declared that the unified nation of Israel would be split in two. God had told Jeroboam that he would rule ten of the tribes (1 Kings 11:29–34). This was God's design, and it showed the consequences of Solomon's sin. The Lord would not allow His people to prosper and be blessed while they were pursuing other gods.

But notice the way in which the Lord allowed the division to happen. Rehoboam was foolish and rejected the wise counsel of his father's advisors while listening to the brash counsel of his friends. Meanwhile, Jeroboam was establishing calves as centers of worship, marking a permanent break between Israel and Judah. Rehoboam's foolishness and Jeroboam's idolatry were both sinful, but they were also the means by which the Lord fulfilled His prophesy that the kingdom would be divided.

This is an important principle to understand: God is in control even when the world seems out of control. In fact, sin and its terrible effects are often the very means God is going to use to bring about His perfect plan. No event in Scripture illustrates this truth as well as the betrayal and crucifixion of Jesus. Pilate was judged for betraying the Prince of Life, but Jesus Himself said that Pilate only had the power to do what God had ordained (John 19:11). Similarly, Judas was judged for betraying Jesus, but this sinful act of betrayal was what led to the death of Christ and the consummation of God's plan of salvation. Of course, this never excuses sin, but it does assure us that God is in control of all things, and all things are working for the glory of God (Romans 11:36).

⌇ Digging Deeper ⌇

5. *Why does God demand moral purity in His followers? How does immorality affect a Christian's influence on others? How does it affect his relationship with God?*

6. *How does understanding God's sovereignty give you confidence in the midst of chaotic and sinful times?*

7. What idols and false gods are followed in America today? Why do people place their faith in them? How do such things fail in the end?

8. What promises have you seen God fulfill in your own life? What promises do you rely on when facing trials or temptation?

⤳ TAKING IT PERSONALLY ⤳

9. Are there any idols in your life? Are you placing your trust in something other than God? What must you do to rid your life of those idols?

10. Are there any areas of impurity in your life? What will you do this week to remove those impurities?

~ 2 ~
THE MINISTRY OF ELISHA

❧ HISTORICAL BACKGROUND ❧

God had ordained one specific tribe in Israel, the descendants of Levi, to be His priests, and only the Levites were eligible for that high calling. Further, the Lord had commanded the Israelites to worship Him in Jerusalem; they were not free to set up temples or shrines on their own, but were constrained to travel to His temple in His chosen city. But Jeroboam, the first king of the Northern Kingdom, had created arbitrary worship sites for the people, scattered around the northern territories of Israel, specifically to prevent the northern tribes from journeying to Jerusalem in Judah. He also disregarded God's commands concerning the priesthood, appointing his own men to serve in that capacity—and they were not from the tribe of Levi.

So God sent prophets to lead His people back into the truth, men who traveled around Israel and Judah preaching the Word of God, urging the people to return to obedience. One such prophet was Elijah, a bold and fiery man who confronted the people, from commoner to king, with the truth of God versus the lies of idolatry. Toward the end of his ministry, the Lord directed Elijah to take Elisha as his servant, acting as a mentor and training Elisha to follow in his footsteps.

But Elisha and Elijah were not working solo (although Elijah may have thought so at times—see 1 Kings 19). In fact, they had established training centers for prophets around Israel to teach men who wanted to study God's Word. Our study opens with Elisha and one of his schools of prophets, a group of godly and committed men who held firm to God's commands.

THE FLASK OF OIL: *A widow approaches Elisha, asking for help in paying an over-whelming debt.*

1. THE SONS OF THE PROPHETS: A group of prophets-in-training who met together for worship and fellowship as they sought to serve the Lord.

YOUR SERVANT MY HUSBAND IS DEAD: According to Jewish tradition, this prophet was Obadiah, who had served the Lord while also working in the court of King Ahab and Queen Jezebel. Jewish writings claim that he had borrowed money to feed the prophets of God when he hid them in caves to preserve their lives from Jezebel's murderous schemes. See the previous book in this series, *A House Divided*, for more information on Obadiah.

THE CREDITOR IS COMING: In ancient times, people in debt could lose more than their property—they could even be taken into slavery for a time. Moreover, it is very likely that her debt was incurred as a result of how her husband cared for the prophets.

2. A JAR OF OIL: This was probably olive oil, which could be used for either food or anointing wounds. It was not an expensive kind of oil.

3. BORROW VESSELS FROM EVERYWHERE: Elijah performed a similar miracle; see 1 Kings 17.

4. SHUT THE DOOR BEHIND YOU: Since the widow's need was private, the provision was to be private also. Further, the absence of Elisha demonstrated that the miracle happened only by God's power. God's power multiplied little into much, filling all the vessels to meet the widow's need.

7. SELL THE OIL: The Lord had blessed the widow far beyond her need. The oil did more than pay off her debt in full; it provided enough to support her and her sons for a long time afterward.

A HOSPITABLE WOMAN: *A couple devotes themselves to serving God's prophet.*

8. SHUNEM: Northwest of Jezreel. (See the map in the Introduction.) Elijah had a very similar relationship with a widow in Zarephath (1 Kings 17).

10. A SMALL UPPER ROOM ON THE WALL: Ancient cities were often surrounded by thick walls, frequently containing small apartments. But this phrase is probably better translated "a walled room on the roof." Typical homes in ancient Israel had flat roofs that were used in many capacities by the family, but they generally did not have separate rooms that were walled off from the rest of the rooftop. The Shunammite couple went to some expense and effort to remodel their home in order to provide Elisha with his own separate living quarters.

BED ... TABLE ... CHAIR ... LAMPSTAND: This godly couple did not hold back on their hospitality to God's prophet, effectively creating a private apartment for him within their home. This would have permitted Elisha to be part of their family for meals, while still maintaining independence and privacy for rest on his journeys. He could come and go as he needed without imposing on his hosts.

11. HE TURNED IN TO THE UPPER ROOM: This suggests that Elisha had complete freedom within the home, allowed to come and go without disturbing the couple. The house was probably built around a square central courtyard that had a staircase going up to the roof. Elisha may have simply entered the house and gone straight up to his apartment.

A GRATEFUL GUEST: *Elisha demonstrates his gratitude to the woman by asking how the Lord can bless her.*

12. GEHAZI: Gehazi is described as Elisha's servant, but it would be more accurate to think of him as a protégé, a prophet in training, with Elisha as his mentor. Elisha enjoyed the same relationship with Elijah—although Gehazi will prove to be vastly different in character from Elisha.

CALL THIS SHUNAMMITE WOMAN: Elisha was not being aloof in sending Gehazi to call the woman, but was more likely seeing whether she was available to speak with him. Elisha also seems to have been giving Gehazi opportunities to minister to people, grooming him for the Lord's work by continuing the conversation with the woman, using Gehazi as a sort of spokesman.

13. WHAT CAN I DO FOR YOU: Elisha demonstrated a spirit of gratitude, recognizing that his hosts had gone to some trouble and expense on his behalf. God calls His people to be both generous hosts and grateful guests.

SPEAK ON YOUR BEHALF TO THE KING: Elisha evidently had access to the king's presence, and he offered to intercede for the couple on any legal matter they might have faced. Since this couple was wealthy and lived in a remote area, bandits were always a danger. Elisha was offering to make sure they were protected by the military.

I DWELL AMONG MY OWN PEOPLE: That is, "I am content with my lot in life." This woman understood a fundamental principle of godliness, which is to learn to be content where the Lord has placed you.

14. WHAT THEN IS TO BE DONE FOR HER: This interaction between Elisha and Gehazi sheds some light on their relationship, which will be useful in a later study. They were conferring together to think up a suitable way of thanking the woman for her great hospitality.

SHE HAS NO SON: In Elijah's time, a childless woman was sometimes viewed as being under God's judgment, and the woman would have keenly felt a sense of unwarranted shame. Her husband also was likely to die without an heir.

16. DO NOT LIE TO YOUR MAIDSERVANT: Elisha's promise touched a deep nerve in the woman's heart, and she recoiled from being deluded with false hopes for something that she longed for so intensely.

17. BUT THE WOMAN CONCEIVED: It seemed impossible to the Shunammite woman that she could become pregnant. She had been barren for many years, and her husband was old and past the normal time of fertility. But God's power is not limited by natural circumstances or timetables, and He never fails to keep His word. Having promised a son through His prophet Elisha, He faithfully delivered. This unnamed woman joined the ranks of other women who gave birth miraculously, including Sarah, Hannah, and most notably, Mary.

A TRAGIC DEATH: *The young boy is suddenly stricken with sickness, and dies in his mother's lap.*

19. MY HEAD, MY HEAD: It is traditionally assumed that the young boy died of sunstroke, although that is not common among people who are accustomed to desert regions. Other maladies have been suggested, but the exact cause of the tragedy remains uncertain.

21. SHE . . . LAID HIM ON THE BED OF THE MAN OF GOD: By placing her son's body on Elisha's bed, this woman showed that she had faith that Elisha's God could raise him from the dead, just as Elijah had done for another widow's son many years earlier (1 Kings 17).

23. IT IS WELL: The mother of the boy apparently concealed the death of the child from her husband to spare him unnecessary grief, in light of the power of the man of God whom she believed might do a miracle for the boy.

25. MOUNT CARMEL: This was the site of Elijah's famous confrontation with the false prophets of Baal many years earlier (1 Kings 18). The distance from Shunem was approximately fifteen to twenty-five miles, or roughly a full day's journey.

26. IT IS WELL: The woman withheld the real sorrow of her son's death, waiting to tell the prophet Elisha directly.

27. SHE CAUGHT HIM BY THE FEET: A gesture both of extreme need and complete reliance on the man of God.

the Lord has hidden it from me: Elisha's great powers of insight and miracles were not due to some psychic ability or magical strength. On the contrary, he was a man, and he depended completely upon the power and revelation of God.

God's Power over Death: *The Lord demonstrates His complete sovereignty, even over death, by raising the son back to life.*

31. The child has not awakened: Elisha had evidently anticipated that the Lord would resurrect the boy when Gehazi placed the staff on his face, understanding that God could use any method He chose to perform His work. A Roman centurion also understood this when he asked Jesus to heal his distant servant simply by speaking (Matthew 8:5–13). In this present case, however, the Lord chose to work in other ways.

34. stretched himself out on the child: Like Elijah in 1 Kings 17, Elisha demonstrated the Lord's power over death by raising their son from the dead. Also like Elijah, part of the restoration process involved Elisha lying on top of the boy's body.

⌁ First Impressions ⌁

1. Elisha instructed the poor widow to close the door to her house. Why didn't he want this miracle to be seen by everyone?

2. What did you learn about God from the way He met the widow's needs? What does this reveal about God's dealings with Christians as individuals?

3. Why did the couple from Shunem construct a special room for Elijah in their house? How did this help Elisha? How did it help the couple? What did it cost the couple?

4. Why did the woman lay her son's body on Elisha's bed? Why did she go to Elisha without telling her husband what had happened? Why wasn't Elisha able to do anything from Mount Carmel?

ᕬ Some Key Principles ᕬ

When we are most needy, God is most gracious.

This section described three situations of dire need: the widow who was on the verge of starvation, the barren woman, and the grieving mother. In each of the three situations, God met the need with His gracious provision. This narrative stresses the fact that our God is a gracious God. He loves to meet His people's needs, because He is faithful.

However, when people rely on their wealth or find their joy in their possessions, they miss the fact that God is capable of meeting their needs. Often we are unable to see and appreciate the graciousness of God unless we first appreciate the depth of our needs. The person who has never experienced hunger does not appreciate the ability of God to miraculously provide food. In times of our greatest need, not only do we turn to God for provision, but we are able to recognize how He is meeting that need.

This same principle applies to our spiritual condition. Only when we realize the depth of our sin can we realize the graciousness of God in salvation. Only when we see how unable we are to save ourselves can we see how gracious God is. This is what Jesus meant when He said, "Those who are well have no need of a physician, but those who are sick. I have not come to call the righteous, but sinners, to repentance" (Luke 5:31–32).

God's people are called to be hospitable.

The woman in this story set an excellent example of hospitality. She knew that Elisha, the Lord's servant, was making regular trips throughout the northern tribes of Israel, tracing a route that took him past her home periodically. She saw a need and met it by providing Elisha with a home away from home. This provision was costly to her and her husband, both financially and personally. They remodeled their home at financial cost to themselves, and they opened up their lives by sharing meals with God's servant.

The book of Hebrews reminds us that we, too, are to share with complete strangers: "Do not forget to entertain strangers, for by so doing some have unwittingly entertained angels" (13:2). Genesis 18 recounts a time when Abraham entertained angels—and even the Lord Himself in a preincarnate appearance. Three strangers arrived at Abraham's camp, and he leaped up to welcome them and to prepare a sumptuous meal for them, little knowing at the time whom he was entertaining. He was tremendously blessed for his hospitality, as the Lord shared His plans for the coming judgment on Sodom and Gomorrah. If Abraham had not been hospitable, he might have missed that blessing.

Jesus taught His disciples that when they showed hospitality to others, they were effectively showing it to Him (Matthew 25:34–40). Peter further instructed his readers, "Be hospitable to one another without grumbling" (1 Peter 4:9). The Shunammite woman provided hospitality without begrudging the cost, and the Lord used this warmth to bless and strengthen His servant Elisha. He also blessed the Shunammite couple, giving them a son in their old age, and miraculously raising him from the dead. Hospitality is a gift that blesses twice, giving to the giver as well as the receiver.

God is in control of life and death.

Elisha faced the timeless dilemma: what to get the woman who had everything. Unlike the widow who was on the verge of starvation, this Shunammite woman had wealth and a husband. But she was barren, and it seems she had given up hope of having a child. Elisha knew that only God can give life, and thus if she received a baby it would be obvious that it was a gift from the Lord.

But when the child died, the Shunammite woman knew this, too, was from the Lord. She did not blame her husband, sickness, or any other factor for the boy's death. Instead she went straight to the man of God. Likewise, Elisha knew the child's death was from the Lord. In fact, it was obvious that no power inherent in Elisha raised the boy to life, rather, it was God who answered Elisha's fervent prayer. Just as the boy's death was from the Lord, so, too, was his new life.

Job, many centuries earlier, lost his children to untimely deaths. When his family was killed by demonically inspired but divinely permitted marauders, Job declared, "The LORD gave, and the LORD has taken away" (Job 1:21). Later he asked his wife, "Shall we indeed accept good from God, and shall we not also accept adversity?" (Job 2:10). Job understood the truth: that all of life is under the control of God. For this reason, we can have confidence in the face of death, but we can also rejoice that our God is the Author of life.

⌁ DIGGING DEEPER ⌁

5. *Why do people see and appreciate God's grace most when they are the most in need? Explain how this is true in both the physical and spiritual realms.*

6.   In Luke 7:47, Jesus said that the person who is forgiven much loves much, while the person who is forgiven little loves little. What do you think Jesus meant by that? How do you see that principle with both the widow and with the Shunammite?

7.   Give some examples of people who have been hospitable to you. What did they do that was helpful? What did it cost them? How were you blessed?

8.   Are there any situations in your life that seem out of control at present? How can you rest in faith that God is in control? How does the knowledge that God is in control help you trust Him?

↪ TAKING IT PERSONALLY ↩

9.   Are you thankful for the daily provision of God in your life right now, or have you started taking it for granted? How can you learn to be more dependent on God for the basics in your life?

10. Spend some time right now making a list of things for which you are thankful. Then spend time every day this week thanking God for these things. Add items to the list as He brings them to mind, and ask Him to teach you contentment.

~ 3 ~
THE KINGSHIP OF ASA

1 KINGS 15; 2 CHRONICLES 14, 16

~ HISTORICAL BACKGROUND ~

King Abijah reigned in Judah for only three years—which proved to be a mercy for the people of Judah. Abijah was not a godly king, and he led the nation of Judah into idolatry and wickedness, just as his father, Rehoboam, had done. As we have already seen, this trend dated back to the reign of Solomon, Abijah's grandfather; and thus far in Judah's history, the old saying has held true: like father, like son.

So we might not have high expectations when Abijah's son Asa takes the throne; after all, three previous generations had led God's people into idol worship, so it is only reasonable to expect the same from the new king. But the Lord is not constrained by a person's lineage and family background; He can choose to use anyone, no matter how unlikely. King Asa, although from a family of compromisers, had his heart changed by God and strove to follow God's Word. The Lord used him to lead Judah away from idolatry and back toward God.

Yet here again we will be confronted with the danger of partial obedience to God. Asa did tear down the pagan high places—but only some of them, not all. That tendency of holding back on obedience would later come back to betray the king, and he would finish his days with a heart that was hardened to the Lord. Nevertheless, Asa is defined in Scripture as a good king, a leader who did what was right in the eyes of the Lord.

~ READING 1 KINGS 15:9–22 ~

KING ASA PURGES FALSE WORSHIP: *Asa, the son of Abijah, takes the throne and begins to walk in obedience to God's Word.*

9. ASA: The son of Abijah, whom we met in Study 1.

10. MAACHAH: We considered Abijah's lineage as an influence on his kingship in Study 1; here we will see that a man can still have his heart turned to the Lord, despite such a heritage.

13. QUEEN MOTHER: Maachah was Asa's grandmother, and she held a place of honor within the king's court. Her functions would have included being an advisor to the king and a teacher of the king's children. In these capacities, she would have exerted a profound influence over national policies and the future kings of Judah.

14. THE HIGH PLACES WERE NOT REMOVED: These were the hilltop sites of pagan worship that the Canaanites had used, and which the people of Israel had never fully destroyed. Solomon reinstated their use by worshiping heathen gods at those sites (1 Kings 11), and they would plague Israel and Judah for the remainder of both kingdoms. Some of the high places were devoted to idolatry, while others were used for a syncretistic blending of paganism with true worship of God. Asa removed some but not all, evidently failing to remove those that blended paganism and truth.

ASA'S HEART WAS LOYAL TO THE LORD: Asa obeyed the Lord for the most part, but stopped short of complete obedience by not purging out the high places. Toward the end of his life, this inclination would cause him problems.

WAR WITH ISRAEL: *King Baasha of Israel tries to besiege Judah. Asa's tactics, however, prove unwise.*

17. RAMAH: King Baasha built this city right on the border between Judah and Israel, just north of Jerusalem. It was situated on a major highway and served to blockade Jerusalem.

19. LET THERE BE A TREATY BETWEEN YOU AND ME: This treaty appeared initially to be a successful political move on Asa's part, but Asa's quickness to negotiate rather than pray and seek deliverance displeased the Lord.

20. THE CITIES OF ISRAEL: This area contained several major trade routes that were vital to Israel. The Chinneroth was the area surrounding the Sea of Galilee. See the gray area on the map in the Introduction for an approximate outline of what was taken by Syria.

22. GEBA . . . MIZPAH: Two cities located north of Jerusalem, near the Israel/Judah border. From a human political perspective, Asa's strategy was very shrewd. His enemy was attacking him at their common border, so he called in allies from the far north to attack his enemy from the rear, taking northern cities away from Israel while Israel's army was busy on its southern border. When the Israelite army withdrew, Asa conscripted the people of Judah into a huge labor force to quickly dismantle his enemy's work and reuse the materials for fortifications against them. The problem, however, was that Asa depended on Syria rather than the Lord to rescue him.

⌁ Reading 2 Chronicles 14:2–15 ⌁

Asa's Faithful Years: *Most of Asa's reign was characterized by a devotion to God's commands, making him one of Judah's good kings.*

2. Asa did what was good and right: The events in this chapter took place prior to Asa's treaty with Syria in the preceding passage.

3. the high places: Asa removed the high places that had been devoted to pagan gods, but he did not remove all the high places that the Israelites had devoted to a blend of right and wrong worship practices.

4. He commanded Judah: Asa understood the role of God's anointed king, which was to lead the people into obedience to God's commands. Too many of Judah's kings did just the opposite, leading God's people into idolatry through their own disobedience. Asa knew that a godly king must lead his subjects by example. He was not perfect, but for the most part he walked in faithfulness to God, and the people followed.

seek ... observe: Notice the deliberate actions that are required of God's people. Seeking involves an intense search for something, while observing entails paying attention to something once it's found. Christians are called to seek the Lord, to search diligently in His Word for an understanding of His character and will. We are also called to observe, to pay attention to His ways as we grow in understanding and maturity—and we must also observe our own lives regularly, being on guard to ensure that we are walking faithfully.

Egypt Attacks: *Egypt sends an army of mercenaries to attack Judah. Asa responds wisely.*

8. shields ... spears ... bows: Notice that the equipment listed does not include chariots. The army from Ethiopia, by contrast, had some three hundred (v. 9). Chariots in ancient battle were equivalent to modern tanks; they were vastly superior in combat against foot soldiers. Asa's army may have outnumbered the Ethiopians, but they were outmatched by the Ethiopians' weapons.

11. it is nothing for You to help: Asa recognized that the Lord could defeat a massive army just as easily as if they were a handful of children. What mattered was not the strength of the foe, but God's ability to answer prayer.

we rest on You: Asa's prayer brings to mind the battle his father fought against Israel, which we considered in Study 1. At that time, the Israelites came prepared to fight, carrying their golden calves. Asa's own faith in God may have been bolstered by that battle, as he saw the Lord defend those who trusted in Him and drive away those who trusted in idols.

13. THEY WERE BROKEN BEFORE THE LORD: The Lord did more than give Judah victory over her enemies; He utterly broke their power. Egypt would not become a world power again for another 150 years.

↜ READING 2 CHRONICLES 16:7–13 ↝

KING ASA'S LATER YEARS: *The Lord sends a prophet to confront Asa about his treaty with Syria, but Asa does not repent.*

7. YOU HAVE RELIED ON THE KING OF SYRIA: We now return to the time when Asa made a treaty with Syria in order to defeat Israel's king Baasha.

NOT RELIED ON THE LORD YOUR GOD: Asa's strategy of bringing the Syrian army in behind his enemy was brilliant from a military perspective, but it showed a lack of trust in God. Asa had placed his faith in Syria's army, and did not act as if the Lord was the leader of Judah's army. The king had seen God's miraculous deliverance against the forces of Egypt and Ethiopia, and he should have called upon the Lord to deliver him from the army of Israel as well.

SYRIA HAS ESCAPED FROM YOUR HAND: Syria was no friend to God's people, and the Lord would have given Asa victory over that nation as well as over Israel, if he had cried out to Him on this occasion as he did previously. As a result, Syria would remain Judah's enemy for a long time to come.

9. THE EYES OF THE LORD: Earlier we saw that Christians should be always seeking the Lord, but it is comforting to find that the Lord is also always seeking those who are willing to be used by Him. He seeks those who are lost to bring them to salvation (Luke 19:10), and He seeks opportunities to show His power and blessings to those who serve Him.

10. ASA WAS ANGRY WITH THE SEER: Sadly, King Asa's heart seems to have grown hard toward the Lord and His commands, and he took out his anger on the Lord's prophet. At some point in his life, Asa evidently began to place his trust in men and armies, rather than in the Lord who alone gives victory. His anger at God's prophet contrasts sharply with King David, who repented of his sin the moment Nathan confronted him (2 Samuel 12).

12. HE DID NOT SEEK THE LORD, BUT THE PHYSICIANS: Asa continued to place his faith in the power and learning of men, rather than in the Lord. This does not mean it is wrong to seek medical help from doctors, but it does remind us that healing comes only from God. One should rely on the Lord for healing, even while seeking human medical attention.

∽ FIRST IMPRESSIONS ∽

1. *Why did Asa remove his grandmother from her position as queen mother? What influence did she have? What did he gain by removing her?*

2. *Why would Asa have removed only some of the high places? What might have motivated him to keep some? How might this apply in your own life?*

3. How did Asa's reign as king compare with that of his father, Abijah, from Study 1? How were the two kings different? What resulted from each man's reign?

4. Why did King Asa command the nation of Judah to seek God? What made this command effective? What made him a godly leader?

↳ Some Key Principles ↰

Place your trust in God, not in man.

King Asa began his reign with an early conflict against an overwhelming foe. An army from Ethiopia came, numbering many times more than the forces of Judah, and they were far better equipped. They evidently were fighting on behalf of Pharaoh, and the people of Judah could well remember the defeat they had suffered the last time Egypt had invaded. But King Asa did not lose heart; he knew that the world's most powerful army could not stand before the hand of God, and in that hour Asa placed his trust openly in God.

Unfortunately, over the years Asa came to place more faith in man than he did in God. He turned to the powerful nation to the north of Israel for help in driving back King Baasha rather than turning to God, as he had done before—even though he faced a far less daunting foe than previously, and despite the fact that Syria was an ungodly nation. When his health failed, he put his trust completely in the learning of men, preferring to turn to human doctors rather than the God who created him.

King Asa should have been warned by the Scriptures: "Do not put your trust in princes, nor in a son of man, in whom there is no help" (Psalm 146:3). The physicians could not cure him, and Syria proved to be a treacherous ally, but God is always faithful and never thwarted. "The LORD is on my side," wrote the psalmist. "I will not fear. What can man do to me? . . . It is better to trust in the LORD than to put confidence in man" (Psalm 118:6, 8).

The godly leader leads by example.

During the early years of his reign, King Asa was a good leader for God's people because he led by example more than by command. It is true that he commanded the people of Judah to seek the Lord and to obey His precepts, but he first set the example by doing it himself. He turned away from the idolatry of his predecessors, removing the very sites where such pagan practices took place. When he was faced with an overwhelming enemy during those early years, he turned to the Lord for protection rather than trusting in the power of his army or in alliances with others.

King David was another king who led by example rather than by command. David's heart was always turned toward the Lord, and he strove throughout his life to be faithful to God's Word. When he did fall into sin, he was quick to repent and confess his sin when a prophet of God confronted him—which was contrary to Asa's response in his later years. Under David, the people of Israel could look to their king for an example of how to lead a godly life, and this is exactly what God intended.

The New Testament teaches the same principle for all those who are in authority. Husbands are called to love their wives as Christ loved the church (Ephesians 5:25); elders are called to lead their flock by living as Jesus lived (1 Timothy 3:1–7). Older men and women are called to live godly lives so that those who are younger might learn by their examples (Titus 2:1–5). In fact, each of us is called to live out the principles of Scripture, regardless of our situations in life, so that we might be a living testimony to the world around us of what it means to be a follower of Christ.

Christians must strive to finish the race well.

King Asa started out strong. He had a heart for God, and strove to obey His commands. He tore down the pagan altars in Judah and purified his own life from the idolatry of his forebears. He trusted fully in the Lord, even when circumstances seemed overwhelming. Unfortunately, he did not finish his reign as he had begun. By the end of his life, he had turned his heart away from trusting the Lord, preferring to place his faith in the wisdom and power of men.

King Solomon followed the same pattern, beginning his reign as a young man who called out to God for wisdom. But as time went along, Solomon's heart was turned away from obedience and toward paganism and idolatry. In both cases, the kings did not persevere in maintaining godliness and purity, and the result was tragic. Nothing is quite as sad as watching a man begin his life strong in his commitment to God, only to sink into worldliness and sin as time goes along.

Paul recognized this tendency in human nature to lose one's focus, and he strove to maintain a strong discipline over the flesh, guarding against those snares and temptations that can gradually lure a person away from God's Word. Comparing the Christian life to a marathon, he wrote: "Do you not know that those who run in a race all run, but one receives the prize? Run in such a way that you may obtain it. And everyone who competes for the prize is temperate in all things. Now they do it to obtain a perishable crown, but we for an imperishable crown. Therefore I run thus: not with uncertainty. Thus I fight: not as one who beats the air. But I discipline my body and bring it into subjection, lest, when I have preached to others, I myself should become disqualified" (1 Corinthians 9:24–27). The wise Christian will always remember to continue in spiritual training, staying the course for the long haul and striving to finish well.

↜ Digging Deeper ↜

5.   *What happened in Asa's later years? What might have caused him to move away from faith in God? How might this principle apply in your own life?*

6. Why did Asa make a treaty with Syria, rather than turning to God as he had done previously? How might this decision have affected his attitude in later years?

7. What is involved in seeking God? In observing His commands? Give practical steps for doing each.

8. What does it mean to rest on God (2 Chronicles 14:11)? How is this done? Why is it important? What is the opposite of resting on God?

⌔ Taking It Personally ⌔

9. How well are you running the Christian race at present? What can you do this week to ensure that you finish the race well?

10. When times of crisis come, where do you instinctively turn for help? Do you generally place your trust more in God or in people?

~ 4 ~
THE KINGSHIP OF JEHOSHAPHAT

2 CHRONICLES 17, 20

⌐ HISTORICAL BACKGROUND ⌐

When King Asa died, his son Jehoshaphat took the throne in Judah. In fact, it is likely that Jehoshaphat reigned alongside his father as co-regent in Judah during the last years of Asa's life, when he was suffering from a severe disease in his feet. Although it didn't end well, Asa's reign had been mostly good, because Asa was generally a godly king. His son, however, was even godlier. King Jehoshaphat was not perfect, of course, and he had a weakness for making bad alliances. One such alliance was with wicked King Ahab, who, together with his evil queen, Jezebel, led Israel into idolatry and murdered God's prophets. Jehoshaphat allied himself with Ahab by marrying his son to Ahab's daughter, then joining with him in a military alliance.

Nevertheless, Jehoshaphat's reign was characterized by godliness and obedience, and the Scriptures declare emphatically that he walked in the ways of David rather than in the sinful ways of Rehoboam and others. Of course, one cannot teach God's Word without first living it out, but Jehoshaphat did this as well. When he was faced with a terrific crisis, as we will see in this study, he did not rely on any of his human alliances, but turned immediately to God for help—and the Lord did not let him down. We will learn, as did Judah, that the battle belongs to God, not to us.

⌐ READING 2 CHRONICLES 17:1–11 ⌐

JEHOSHAPHAT, A GODLY KING: *Asa's son Jehoshaphat takes the throne, and he leads Judah in the ways of God.*

1. JEHOSHAPHAT: The son of Asa. Jehoshaphat and his father probably reigned together as co-regents during the last few years of Asa's illness. His name means "Jehovah has judged."

2. HE PLACED TROOPS IN ALL THE FORTIFIED CITIES OF JUDAH: Jehoshaphat ruled Judah during turbulent times, when the nation faced enemies in every direction—

including their own kinsman of Israel immediately to the north. This was, therefore, prudent leadership, and the nation of Judah enjoyed a season of peace. It is important to note, however, that the peace was due to the neighboring nations experiencing "the fear of the LORD" (v. 10), not the fear of Judah's military might.

3. THE LORD WAS WITH JEHOSHAPHAT, BECAUSE: That word *because* is very significant in this verse. As we have seen several times already, the Lord promises to be with His people *if* they seek Him and observe His commands. This does not mean that a person earns God's favor by doing good deeds. God's favor cannot be earned by any person or by any means; it is given solely by God's grace. Nevertheless, a person who has been redeemed must live in fellowship with the Lord if he wants to experience the full presence and blessing of God in his life.

THE FORMER WAYS OF HIS FATHER DAVID: David's life was characterized by a steadfast determination to walk according to God's Word. David sinned, as did subsequent kings, but David was quick to repent of his sin and turn back to the Lord.

6. HIS HEART TOOK DELIGHT: This is the first time that any king since the division of Israel and Judah had been described as one who delighted in God's way. The phrase could be literally translated "his soul was exalted." This suggests that Jehoshaphat found pleasure in obeying God's Word, and the process enriched his entire being.

7. HE SENT HIS LEADERS . . . TO TEACH: Asa had commanded the people of Judah to seek God, but Jehoshaphat went a step further and taught the people from God's Word. This was God's original intention for the leaders of Israel at every level: that they instruct others in the Word of God (Deuteronomy 6:6–9). Making God's commandments the law of the land forces a nation to live by godly principles, but teaching the people His Word permits them to love Him of their own free will.

10. THE FEAR OF THE LORD: It is significant that the author of 2 Chronicles mentioned this fact in conjunction with the widespread teaching of God's Word, not with the fortification of Judah's cities. Ironically, when the people of Judah turned their hearts to God's Word, the Lord caused the neighboring nations to fear them, making the military superfluous.

⤳ READING 2 CHRONICLES 20:1–30 ⤶

BETRAYAL: *Judah is suddenly attacked by three armies, nations that the Israelites had treated well.*

1. AFTER THIS: King Jehoshaphat had made an alliance with King Ahab in Israel by marrying his son to Ahab's daughter, then joining forces to fight against Ramoth Gilead. This alliance brought God's wrath on the house of Jehoshaphat, resulting in dire results after Jehoshaphat's death. See 2 Chronicles 18–19 for a full account; also see the previous book in this series, *A House Divided*, for a deeper look at the alliance.

MOAB ... AMMON: Canaanite neighbors to the east of Judah and Israel, respectively. See the map in the Introduction.

3. JEHOSHAPHAT FEARED: In this case, fear was the normal human reaction to the grave threat that had materialized suddenly. But Jehoshaphat did not permit his fear to control him; instead, he immediately turned to the Lord for help.

SET HIMSELF TO SEEK THE LORD: That is, he devoted himself to prayer and fasting, committing all his time and energy to calling upon the Lord. As king, he must have had many pressing concerns and obligations, and he certainly had urgent business to attend to with an invading army at his doorstep—but Jehoshaphat set aside all those distractions and concentrated his heart and mind on prayer.

JEHOSHAPHAT'S PRAYER: *The king comes before the Lord with an urgent plea, placing the battle in God's hands.*

6. YOU ... RULE OVER ALL THE KINGDOMS OF THE NATIONS: Jehoshaphat recognized the fact that kings and rulers—even sinful ones—reign under the will and authority of God. God will judge sinful leaders for their actions, but in the end, a nation stands or falls solely according to God's will.

7. DROVE OUT THE INHABITANTS OF THIS LAND: As we have already noted, the Lord expelled the Canaanites because they had devoted themselves to false gods. Israel was following the same course at this time, but under Jehoshaphat's leadership the nation of Judah had turned away from idolatry—for a time. In the end, both Israel and Judah would be driven out of Canaan for the same reason.

10. AMMON, MOAB, AND MOUNT SEIR: The Ammonites and Moabites were descendants of Lot (Abraham's nephew), and the descendants of Esau (Jacob's twin brother) lived in Mount Seir. The Lord had specifically instructed Israel to not fight against these nations when they were leaving Egypt for Canaan (Deuteronomy 2), but to treat them with respect. Jehoshaphat was reminding the Lord in his prayer that Judah and Israel had gone out of their way to be at peace with these people, and now their kindness was being betrayed.

12. WE HAVE NO POWER: This was a recurring lesson for the people of Judah, recognizing that they had no power in themselves to control the future or to subdue their enemies. The godly kings, such as Jehoshaphat, understood this and turned to the Lord for protection when threatened by destruction; but ungodly kings, such as Rehoboam and Abijah, tried to solve their problems through their own strength—or worse, by turning to man-made idols.

OUR EYES ARE UPON YOU: This is the first step in seeking God: to be keeping one's eyes upon Him. This is done by studying His Word, asking His will in prayer, and obeying His direction in daily action.

13. WITH THEIR LITTLE ONES, THEIR WIVES, AND THEIR CHILDREN: Walking with God is a family matter, and a believer's children should be included in the entire process. The Lord had commanded the Israelites to teach His Word to their children from their earliest years (Deuteronomy 6:6–9), training them how to walk in obedience when they were young so they would have wisdom when they came to lead their own families.

THE LORD'S RESPONSE: *The Lord sends a prophet to the people of Judah, instructing them on what to do.*

15. DO NOT BE AFRAID NOR DISMAYED: Fear is a natural response to danger, but it can also become a debilitating danger in itself. God's Word frequently exhorts believers to resist fear and to be courageous. Verse 3 tells us that Jehoshaphat was afraid when he heard of the coming invasion, but he also demonstrated how one overcomes fear: by turning to the Lord in prayer.

THE BATTLE IS NOT YOURS, BUT GOD'S: Once again, the Lord reminded His people that He was their sole source of security against this world's threats. God wants His children to depend on Him for everything, rather than on their own devices. This is not a passive process, however; we must be actively walking in obedience and faith, and the Lord frequently calls us to participate in His plans—but the ultimate direction and outcome of those plans are entirely in His hands.

16. GO DOWN AGAINST THEM: Here is an example of the above principle: the Lord had declared that the battle was entirely His, yet He also wanted His people to be involved. They were not to sit at home, passively waiting for God to destroy their enemies. They had a role to play, and the Lord insisted they do their part.

THEY WILL SURELY COME UP BY THE ASCENT OF ZIZ: When a believer turns the battle over to God's control, he gains an omniscient Commander in Chief. The Lord never needs to speculate or strategize, for He knows all things in advance. No human leader could ever hope to stand before God's wisdom and power.

17. POSITION YOURSELVES, STAND STILL AND SEE: Here is some practical instruction on how to turn a battle over to God's control. To position oneself is to take a deliberate and public stand, making a firm determination that one belongs to God. To stand still requires one to stop fighting, to cease from one's own attempts to control or conquer. When a believer determines to allow God to control a situation and stops fighting in his own power, he will invariably see God's faithfulness and sovereignty—and he will ultimately see great victory.

GO OUT AGAINST THEM: It is significant that the Lord commanded His people to not fight, then commanded them to go out against the foe as though to war. It is true that the Lord would fight the battle, but the people of Judah also had a part in the conflict. Their share in the battle was to stand firm and sing God's praises. It may have seemed an insignificant role to the people, but it was an integral part of the battle plan nonetheless.

PREPARING FOR BATTLE: *The people of Judah gather in preparation for war—by singing praises to God.*

18. WORSHIPING THE LORD: This was an open act of faith, as the people of Judah praised and worshiped the Lord before the battle even began. God had promised a victory, and the people believed Him, knowing that He always keeps His promises.

19. WITH VOICES LOUD AND HIGH: The people's worship was very open and public, and they didn't hold back in singing God's praises. This was an important public testimony for the world around them, as well as an encouragement to the people of Judah as they prepared to face a powerful foe.

22. THE LORD SET AMBUSHES: God might have sent angels to create confusion and mayhem among the enemy, or He might have simply used the natural distrust that these three nations had for one another. Ammon and Moab were descendants of Lot and were thus a sort of national cousins, while Esau's descendants from Mount Seir would have been like outsiders. However the Lord accomplished it, the rout was similar to His miraculous preservation of Israel during Gideon's day (Judges 7).

24. THERE WERE THEIR DEAD BODIES: The people of Judah marched out to battle, but the war was over before they got there! They did not have to do anything but gather up the spoils.

28. TO THE HOUSE OF THE LORD: The ordeal ended where it began, at the house of God. The people of Judah did not forget to praise and thank the Lord for answering their prayers, an important step in our relationship with God.

↳ First Impressions ↵

1. What made Jehoshaphat a good king? How did his reign compare with Asa's? With Rehoboam's?

2. Why did Jehoshaphat send leaders into Judah to teach the people? How did this differ from Asa's approach? How is Jehoshaphat's approach superior?

3. Why did the prophet Jahaziel command the people to "not be afraid nor dismayed" (2 Chronicles 20:15)? How might fear have hindered the people of Judah from trusting God?

4. *What did God mean when He commanded the people to position themselves, stand still, and see (2 Chronicles 20:17)? How are these things done?*

✦ Some Key Principles ✦

The battle belongs to God—but we also have a role to play.

Jehoshaphat recognized that his people were powerless to defeat the terrible foe that came to destroy them, and he turned to the Lord. This was exactly the right response, for the Lord wants His people to let Him fight their battles, and God promised the king that He would rout the foe—"for the battle is not yours," said Jahaziel, "but God's" (2 Chronicles 20:15).

Nevertheless, this promise did not give the people of Judah the right to go home and take a nap until the war was over. The Lord was indeed going to do the fighting for them, but they still had a part to play in the conflict. It was not an aggressive part; on the contrary, their role was to take a position, stand firm in it, and watch. Their position was to trust that the Lord would keep His promises, then to stand firm in that faith even though they were faced with an overwhelming foe that threatened to destroy them. By standing firm in their faith, they were free to watch for God's great deliverance—and when it came, they saw that their faith was not in vain.

This is what it means to stand strong in the faith. We have the steadfast assurance that God will always keep His promises, and we can fully depend on Him to protect us and fight on our behalf against the enemy who seeks to destroy us. When we are firm in our faith, we can see God work in our lives for His glory, and we can also realize that all of the glory belongs to God. He will deliver us, and we will surely see that our faith is not in vain.

Obedience produces blessing.

The Scriptures make it clear that sin has negative consequences. When a person lives in sin, he incurs not only divine chastisement and displeasure but also the temporal negative consequences of sin. But obedience has consequences as well: it produces blessing in a person's life.

As an example of this principle, the author of 2 Chronicles tells us that "the LORD was with Jehoshaphat, because he walked in the former ways of his father David; he did not seek the Baals, but sought the God of his father, and walked in His commandments and not according to the acts of Israel" (17:3–4). Jehoshaphat obeyed the Lord, and thus experienced the blessing of divine pleasure.

It is not really that Jehoshaphat's obedience *caused* God's blessing; it would be more accurate to say that obedience came with God's blessing. In other words, blessing was the result of Jehoshaphat's obedience. When a person obeys God, he experiences not only divine approval but also the joy of walking with the Lord.

When we deliberately disregard God's commands, we cheat ourselves and hinder His work in our lives. "If you keep My commandments," Jesus taught, "you will abide in My love, just as I have kept My Father's commandments and abide in His love" (John 15:10). When we abide in His love, we receive the fullness of the Father's blessings in our lives, and we grow ever more in Christ's image.

The godly leader teaches others from God's Word.

Jehoshaphat's kingship, for the most part, was a model of godly leadership. His father Asa had commanded the people of Judah to observe and obey the Word of God, and this was good. But Jehoshaphat actively *instructed* the people in God's Word, and this was even better. He understood that enforced obedience might cause a nation to outwardly obey God's commands, but it did not cause an inward transformation of love and worship on the people's part. The first step in that process comes from understanding of the Word of God.

God calls all of us to various levels of authority, whether in the home, the church, the workplace, or the community, and He wants us to be teaching others from His Word. This is accomplished first and foremost through our example, and in this sense each Christian has the authority to teach by example to the world around him. Yet our teaching should extend beyond outward obedience to include actively telling others the truth of Jesus Christ. This can be illustrated within a godly home, as parents—and especially fathers—are commanded by God to teach their children from God's Word on a regular basis.

Jesus, of course, is the perfect example of this principle. He lived a sinless life, completely obeying all that His Father commanded Him, and His life was a living epistle of God's truth to the world around. Yet Jesus did not stop with obedience—even perfect obedience; He coupled His walk with His words, openly teaching God's truth to all who would listen. This is what Jesus commanded His disciples to do: "Go therefore and make disciples of all the nations . . . teaching them to observe all things that I have commanded you" (Matthew 28:19–20). The godly leader will follow Jesus' example, both living and teaching the Word of God.

↶ DIGGING DEEPER ↷

5. What does it mean that Jehoshaphat's "heart took delight in the ways of the LORD" (2 Chronicles 17:6)? How is this done? What are the results?

6. What role did music and praise play in Judah's battle? What role did worship play? How are these things important to resting in faith?

7. In your own words, what exactly does it mean to stand strong in the faith? How is this done? What are the results?

8. *What godly teachers have influenced your life? How did they couple godly behavior with teaching words? How might you imitate their examples?*

↳ TAKING IT PERSONALLY ↲

9. *What battles is the Lord calling you to turn over to Him at present? How will you do that? What steps will you take this week to rest in faith?*

10. *Is there an area of deliberate disobedience in your life? What will you do today to turn away from that sinful behavior?*

5
EXILE

⌒ HISTORICAL BACKGROUND ⌒

King David's son Solomon had ascended the throne over a united Israel in 971 BC, but forty years later the nation was torn in two. For the next two hundred years, the northern tribes of Israel were ruled by a succession of kings, the vast majority of whom were not faithful to God's commands. During those years, Israel became increasingly idolatrous, until it was virtually indistinguishable from the pagan nations around it.

The books of Kings and Chronicles cover a period of more than four hundred years, and during those years there were great fluctuations in world power, as one would expect. Egypt and Assyria wrestled back and forth for dominance, and both were eventually overshadowed by Babylon (modern-day Iraq), which itself would later be overshadowed by Persia (modern-day Iran). In 725 BC, the Assyrians besieged Samaria, and three years later the nation of Israel was taken into captivity. While Judah continued to exist for 140 more years, eventually she, too, became as wicked as Israel. In 605 BC, Babylon's king Nebuchadnezzar forced Judah into subservience, carrying away a number of her young men into captivity—one of whom was Daniel. King Zedekiah, the ruler of Judah, subsequently rebelled against Nebuchadnezzar, so the Babylonians returned and utterly destroyed Judah in 586 BC, carrying the remaining people into captivity. Israel's days as a nation came to an inglorious and tragic ending.

This is a sad study, as we watch God's people falling into depravity and being carried away to slavery in foreign lands. Yet even in the midst of Israel's darkest hour, we discover God's mercy and grace in remembering His promises to His people. After seventy years of captivity, the Lord would move the heart of Cyrus, Persia's king, and His people would return to Jerusalem.

↜ Reading 2 Kings 17:7–23 ↝

The Sins of Israel: *For more than a hundred years, the people of Israel have been chasing after foreign gods. The Lord's patience has come to an end.*

8. walked in the statutes of the nations: This included idolatry and pagan worship in the high places, but it also included other abominations, such as child sacrifice and astrology. Israel, as we shall see, was guilty of practically every atrocity that the Canaanites had practiced before Israel's arrival in the promised land—and for which the Lord had driven out the Canaanites in the first place. That same fate was now coming upon the northern tribes of Israel.

and of the kings of Israel: As we have seen, Israel's king Jeroboam attempted to rewrite God's prescribed worship practices in Israel. He led the people to worship the Lord at a variety of sites around Israel, rather than in Jerusalem, as the Lord had commanded, and he added an idolatrous element to their worship by introducing the golden calves. The people of Israel were guilty of open idolatry, and also of syncretism—the sin of mixing pagan practices into legitimate worship of God.

9. Israel secretly did . . . things: The Hebrew word translated *secretly* literally means "to cover." The people of Israel thought they could hide their wicked deeds from the Lord, as though such a thing were possible.

10. sacred pillars and wooden images: The wooden images were carved representations of false gods, while the pillars were fertility objects used during rituals involving sexual immorality. These objects of wickedness were spread throughout the northern tribes and found "on every high hill and under every green tree."

11. like the nations whom the Lord had carried away before them: Once again, we are reminded that the Lord drove out the Canaanites from the land for these very same practices. If He drove out the Canaanites for such wickedness, He would surely also drive out the Israelites.

The Lord's Long-suffering: *Despite His people's sin, the Lord continued to send prophets urging them to repentance.*

12. You shall not do this thing: See Exodus 20:3–5.

13. Turn from your evil ways: Despite the widespread paganism in Israel, the Lord continued to show patience and mercy, giving His people many opportunities to repent. He also sent prophets to Israel and Judah, never leaving them without spiritual guidance, urging them continuously to turn away from idolatry and back to Him. But Israel would not obey.

14. STIFFENED THEIR NECKS: The people became obstinate, insisting upon doing things their own way regardless of what God commanded. We will see in later studies that the people also hardened their hearts.

15. THEY REJECTED HIS STATUTES AND HIS COVENANT: The Lord had clearly taught His people how to worship Him and live according to His will through the teachings of His prophets, including Moses, and the covenants He had made, which promised them blessings if they obeyed His commands. Yet they preferred to imitate the world around them. The church today is in danger of doing the same thing, as many attempt to incorporate all manner of worldly values and ideas into their worship practices under the cloak of being "relevant" to the world around them. In reality, such syncretism only makes the church worldly, not relevant.

THEY SHOULD NOT DO LIKE THEM: God commanded His people to be different from the world. If God's church is just like every other worldly organization, then the unsaved have no reason to go there. Paradoxically, it is our very difference from the world around us that draws sinners to Christ, for only then can they see that God alone is the source of salvation.

16. TWO CALVES . . . WOODEN IMAGE . . . THE HOST OF HEAVEN: Jeroboam had led Israel to worship the golden calves (1 Kings 12:25–33), while Rehoboam had built the wooden image (1 Kings 14:15). The people also committed the sin of astrology, looking to the stars for guidance instead of to God's Word.

17. TO PASS THROUGH THE FIRE: The Canaanites believed in a god named Molech, whose worship included sacrificing children in the fire.

WITCHCRAFT AND SOOTHSAYING: Witchcraft includes the sin of attempting to contact the spirit world and to use magic to control the natural realm. Soothsaying is the sin of divination, endeavoring to use magical means to foretell the future. Latent in this is the idea that the dead can guide better than God's Word.

SOLD THEMSELVES TO DO EVIL: This phrase captures the very essence of sin. Esau sold his birthright to Jacob in exchange for a bowl of stew; Adam sold himself into slavery to sin and death in exchange for a piece of fruit. In the same way, men and women sell their very souls in exchange for worthless, momentary pleasures. Sin is always a bad bargain.

᜔ READING 2 CHRONICLES 36:11–23 ᜔

THE FALL OF JUDAH: *The nation of Judah walked in intermittent faithfulness to the Lord, but approximately 135 years after Israel's fall, Judah goes into captivity.*

11. ZEDEKIAH: This was the last king of Judah; see page 54 for a complete list. Jeremiah prophesied during Zedekiah's reign (Jeremiah 1:3) and wrote the book of Lamentations to mourn the destruction of Jerusalem and the temple.

13. KING NEBUCHADNEZZAR: Nebuchadnezzar was the king of Babylon, which was located in what we know today as Iraq. Zedekiah apparently swore an oath of allegiance to Nebuchadnezzar, but a man who rebels against God will not hesitate to rebel against earthly authorities, which Zedekiah did here as well.

14. TRANSGRESSED MORE AND MORE: Sin breeds more sin, just as rebellion breeds further rebellion. The leaders and the people fell deeper and deeper into sin, defiling the temple with pagan practices.

15. RISING UP EARLY AND SENDING THEM: That is, He sent His messengers early and late, again and again, persistently warning the people of His coming wrath if they did not turn back to Him.

16. THEY MOCKED THE MESSENGERS OF GOD: There is nothing new about the world mocking God's messengers; we certainly see that today in the popular media and elsewhere. But this verse is not referring to the world; it is referring to the people of God, as they themselves had mocked God's messengers, despised His Word, and scoffed at His prophets—the very agents God was trying to use to save them from wrath.

TILL THERE WAS NO REMEDY: It is important to recognize that God's patience and mercy do not continue indefinitely when a nation or individual refuses to repent. The time of judgment will come, and when it arrives, there will be no remedy, no second chance, no further opportunity for repentance.

17. THE KING OF THE CHALDEANS: That is, Nebuchadnezzar. The Chaldeans were from Babylon. Under Nebuchadnezzar, they became the primary world power, and the city of Babylon was one of the wonders of the ancient world.

19. THEY BURNED THE HOUSE OF GOD: This act marked the end for the nations of Judah and Israel, as it demonstrated that God had removed His presence from His holy city of Jerusalem. He had not abandoned His people, but when His Spirit left the temple it was an expression that the people had abandoned Him. The Lord would leave them in captivity for seventy years.

21. UNTIL THE LAND HAD ENJOYED HER SABBATHS: The Lord had commanded His people to observe a Sabbath of the land every seven years. In that seventh year, the people were to not grow any crops, permitting the land to rest (Leviticus 25:1–7). Apparently, the Israelites had not obeyed this command for 490 years, meaning they had missed seventy Sabbaths for their land. Their seventy-year exile gave the land the rest that it was owed.

23. LET HIM GO UP: After seventy years of captivity, the Lord moved Cyrus of Persia to release some of His people to return to Jerusalem. See the next book in this series, *God's Presence During Hardship*, for more information on this time period.

⤵ FIRST IMPRESSIONS ⤴

1. What does it mean to walk "in the statutes of the nations" (2 Kings 17:8)? What are some statutes of modern nations that differ from the Word of God?

2. What does it mean that the people of Israel "stiffened their necks" against the Lord? How does a person become stiff-necked? How does one stop being stiff-necked?

3. Why does God view divination as such an extreme example of sin? When someone turns to those things for guidance, what does that say about their trust in God's Word?

4. *Why would a parent make the choice to sacrifice his son or daughter to an idol? How does this sin compare with the modern notion of abortion?*

⌁ Some Key Principles ⌁

God's judgment is coming.

The Lord endured the unfaithfulness of His people for many years. Both Israel and Judah committed all manner of wickedness, chasing after gods that didn't exist and imitating the pagan nations around them, yet the Lord stayed His hand of judgment. Even more, He continually sent prophets and teachers to call the people to repentance and teach them the true ways of righteousness. Yet God's people rejected those prophets, mocking them and imprisoning them and murdering them—all the time persisting in their idolatrous practices.

The prophets warned both Israel and Judah that the Lord's wrath would come upon them if they did not repent, but the people did not believe. As we have considered in previous studies, the Lord always keeps His promises—and this includes vows of coming judgment. After several hundred years of stubborn indulgence in sin, the Lord's people were driven out of Canaan. This was a terrific tragedy: countless Israelites were slaughtered, while those who survived faced slavery and hardship for the rest of their days—yet no one in either Israel or Judah could accuse God of treachery, for He had warned them again and again of the judgment that would come if they did not repent.

We live today in the age of God's grace, but we must never forget that the age of grace will come to an end—and it will be followed by God's final judgment upon the sinfulness of mankind. The captivity and suffering of Israel were nothing compared to the coming judgment, when those who have refused to repent will be cast into outer darkness—not for a lifetime but for all eternity. Those who have accepted God's gift of salvation through Christ will not face that judgment, yet even Christians must never take God's grace for granted or test His patience with continual sin. Paul had this in mind when he urged his readers, "We . . . plead with you not to receive the grace of God in vain. For He says: 'In an acceptable time I have heard you, and in the day of salvation I have helped you.' Behold, now is the accepted time; behold, now is the day of salvation" (2 Corinthians 6:1–2).

God sees all things, and nothing is done in secret.

The people of Israel and Judah grew bold in their idolatries, carrying out their false worship on open hilltops and public groves, and these rites frequently included all sorts of evil. But they did not limit their sinful behaviors to the idolatrous ceremonies; they carried their spiritual rebellion into the most secret areas of their private lives. They were undoubtedly able to hide such things from their friends and neighbors, but they were foolish in thinking they could keep them secret from the Lord.

The Israelites may also have covered their sins in a cloak of respectability, using false logic to argue that their sin wasn't actually sin at all. Mankind is very skilled in such sophistry, able to justify every sinful deed to the point of calling evil good and good evil. But God hates such a mind-set, as He warned us through the prophet Isaiah: "Woe to those who call evil good, and good evil; who put darkness for light, and light for darkness; who put bitter for sweet, and sweet for bitter!" (Isaiah 5:20).

There is nothing hidden from God's sight, and that includes both our deeds and our elaborate excuses to justify our sins. Paul wrote that the Lord "will both bring to light the hidden things of darkness and reveal the counsels of the hearts" (1 Corinthians 4:5). When we remember that God sees our hearts and our secret actions, we are more apt to walk circumspectly, and more quick to confess our sins. But when we try to keep those sins secret, we act foolishly, "for there is nothing covered that will not be revealed, nor hidden that will not be known" (Luke 12:2).

Occult activities are an attempt to replace God.

The idolatry of Israel and Judah began as syncretism, a blending of pagan ideas with the true worship of God—but it ended with the most hideous abominations, including child sacrifice. This was a clear testimony that the Israelites thought their own God was insufficient to guide them. They thought they needed protection and direction from other gods. While child sacrifice may sound like an extreme case, the fact is that all disobedience to God's Word eventually leads to abominable practices if the person does not repent and turn away from disobedience. By definition, sin is the act of choosing to follow inner desires rather than submitting to God, and all sin leads inexorably away from the Lord and toward evil.

Interestingly, the Lord includes child sacrifice in the category of occult abominations. Today this is practiced through the widespread sin of abortion. It is no coincidence that as Western civilization hardens its heart against God, sins like this are becoming more accepted.

Christians, of course, must have no part in such sins. God strictly forbade His people to even associate with "anyone who makes his son or his daughter pass through the fire, or one who practices witchcraft, or a soothsayer, or one who interprets omens, or a sorcerer, or one who conjures spells, or a medium, or a spiritist, or one who calls up the dead. For all who do these things are an abomination to the LORD, and because of these abominations the LORD your God drives them out from before you" (Deuteronomy 18:10–12). As Christians, our direction and protection is found in the Lord, and not through other means, such as the sacrifice of children.

↜ DIGGING DEEPER ↝

5. *What does it mean to sell oneself to do evil (2 Kings 17:17)? How does this happen? How does one prevent it?*

6. *What did God do to prevent His people from losing the promised land? What did the people do to thwart Him? What was the result?*

7. Why does God hate the occult? Why does He forbid His people to even associate with those who practice such things?

8. In what ways does sin breed more sin? When have you seen this in your own life? What is the solution to breaking out of that cycle?

⤳ Taking It Personally ⤶

9. Are you saved from the coming final judgment of God? Are you trusting in your own righteousness or the righteousness of Jesus Christ to reconcile you to God? Understand that you can be forgiven by turning to Christ as your Savior and Lord through repentance and faith.

10. Are you harboring secret sins in your life? What false reasoning do you use to justify such sins? Are you willing to openly confess those things to the Lord today?

The Kings of Judah*

Ruler	Reign (BC)**	Length (years)
Saul	1050–1010	40
David	1010–970	40
Solomon	970–930	40
Rehoboam	931–913	17
Abijam (Abijah)	913–911	3
Asa	911–870	41
Jehoshaphat	870 (873)–848	25
Jehoram (Joram)	848 (853)–841	8
Ahaziah (Jehoahaz)	841	1
Queen Athaliah	841–835	6
Joash (Jehoash)	835–796	40
Amaziah	796–767	29
Uzziah (Asariah)	767 (792)–740	52
Jotham	740 (750)–731	16
Ahaz	731 (735)–715	16
Hezekiah	715 (729)–686	29
Manasseh	686 (696)–642	55
Amon	642–640	2
Josiah	640–609	31
Jehoahaz (Shallum)	609	(3 months)
Jehoiakim (Eliakim)	609–598	11
Jehoiachin (Coniah)	598–597	(3 months)
Zedekiah (Mattaniah)	597–586	11
Judah enters captivity	586	

*For the kings of Israel, see the previous book in this series, *A House Divided*.

**Dates in parentheses indicate a co-regency of father and son. Dates are approximate.

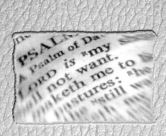

SECTION 2:

CHARACTERS

In This Section:

~ 6 ~
ELISHA

↝ CHARACTER'S BACKGROUND ↜

We now return to the time before Israel went into captivity, approximately 125 years prior to that tragic event. King Ahab had died, and his son Jehoram was king in his place (preceded very briefly by Ahaziah, another son of Ahab). The king of Judah was also named Jehoram, the son of Jehoshaphat. Israel's old enemy Syria was still actively working to destroy God's people. The two nations were not engaged in an all-out war, but Syria was continually carrying out raids and skirmishes on Israel's soil.

Meanwhile, Elijah had grown old in service to the Lord, and the time of his departure was at hand. But by "departure" we do not mean death, for the Lord had revealed to Elijah that he would not die but would instead be translated directly into heaven, in bodily form. His servant Elisha was already appointed by God to carry on his mentor's great ministry, yet Elisha may have felt some concern about his ability to walk in Elijah's footsteps. He lived in troubled times, and he may well have felt inadequate to the daunting task ahead. Nevertheless, Elisha knew where Elijah's power came from, and he made a very bold final request of his mentor before their parting: a double portion of Elijah's spirit. The Lord granted his request and demonstrated His mighty power in many dramatic ways, as we will see in this study.

↝ READING 2 KINGS 2:1–22 ↜

ELIJAH'S FAREWELL TOUR: *Elijah and Elisha travel to the schools of prophets one more time so Elijah can say good-bye.*

1. THE LORD WAS ABOUT TO TAKE UP ELIJAH: These events took place during the reigns of King Ahab in Israel and King Jehoshaphat in Judah.

ELIJAH WENT WITH ELISHA: The Lord had directed Elijah to appoint Elisha as his successor, training him to take his mantle of leadership—quite literally, as it turned out— and preparing him to be a prophet to God's people during a time of growing apostasy.

2. STAY HERE: Elijah made this request of Elisha three times, and three times Elisha steadfastly refused. It is possible that Elijah was merely suggesting that Elisha remain and minister at one of the schools of prophets, permitting Elijah to depart alone. What Elijah discovered was that Elisha was determined to take on his mentor's difficult and lonely ministry. Elisha needed to be present when Elijah was taken to heaven if he were to receive a double portion of God's Spirit (vv. 9–10), yet Elijah also knew the cost of his ministry. Elisha showed that despite Elijah encouraging him to stay behind, he was prepared to pay that cost.

I WILL NOT LEAVE YOU: Elisha demonstrated a firm resolve to be faithful to his mentor, and nothing could shake him from it. He held the same resolve toward God's commands, making him a fitting successor to Elijah.

3. KEEP SILENT: Elisha's stern response suggests that the sons of the prophets may have been expressing some excitement at knowing what was going to happen to Elijah. If so, Elisha felt that such voyeurism was inappropriate; this was a day of sadness, because Elijah was going to depart from them. Elisha was undoubtedly somewhat heavyhearted at the prospect of saying good-bye to his beloved teacher and friend, and any lighthearted chatter would have been unwelcome.

CROSSING THE JORDAN: *Elijah and Elisha cross the Jordan, and God parts the waters miraculously.*

8. STRUCK THE WATER: Moses similarly struck the Nile with his rod when the Israelites were still in Egypt, turning the water to blood (Exodus 7:14–25). This was a public demonstration that God's power was with Elijah. This demonstration of God's power would be used later by Elisha.

9. A DOUBLE PORTION: Elisha was asking for the spiritual birthright, comparable to the double portion of inheritance that went to a man's firstborn son. He was essentially asking to become Elijah's spiritual successor as leader of the prophets and a spokesman for God. It is interesting that Scripture records twice as many miracles through Elisha as through Elijah, but this was not what Elisha was requesting. His main concern was that he needed Elijah's mighty power if he was going to accomplish what the Lord was calling him to do.

10. YOU HAVE ASKED A HARD THING: Elijah's life was hard: he was persecuted, arrested, scorned, abused, and hated. This was not a life that Elijah wanted someone he loved to have to endure. Moreover, Elijah himself was powerless to grant Elisha's request. He knew that if the Lord intended to say yes to Elisha, He would permit him to witness Elijah's ascent to heaven as a sign.

Chariots of Fire: *The two prophets are deep in conversation, when suddenly the Lord's messengers appear and carry Elijah to heaven.*

11. AS THEY CONTINUED ON AND TALKED: The Lord's appearing to whisk away Elijah was sudden and without warning, even though both of the prophets were expecting it. In the same way, the Lord Himself will descend with a shout to catch up His people from the earth, taking all believers to be with Him forever (1 Thessalonians 4:16–17). Like Enoch's departure (Genesis 5:24), this is a stunning picture of how God can take His children from the earth. Enoch and Elijah did not die; they were transformed.

A CHARIOT OF FIRE: The chariot was the most powerful weapon of warfare in Elijah's day. The most fearsome chariots were made of wood and reinforced with iron, generally drawn by a team of trained war horses. But God's chariot and horses were made of fire, giving a vivid picture to Elisha that His power and majesty exceed anything that the world is capable of producing.

ELIJAH WENT UP BY A WHIRLWIND INTO HEAVEN: Elijah and Enoch (Genesis 5:24) are the only two men recorded to have been taken bodily into heaven without experiencing death. We are not told why the Lord chose to do this, yet a whirlwind and chariot of fire provided an apt conclusion to Elijah's fiery ministry.

12. THE CHARIOT OF ISRAEL AND ITS HORSEMEN: Israel's strength and welfare lay in God's hands, not in the nation's military might. God was taking away His representative from Israel, and Elisha implied that a nation without God's leadership was left defenseless. The Lord was not removing His prophets entirely, however, as Elisha would soon demonstrate.

13. THE MANTLE OF ELIJAH: There was nothing unusual about Elijah's cloak, and it contained no special powers. Elisha's use of it merely identified him to the sons of the prophets as Elijah's successor.

14. WHERE IS THE LORD GOD OF ELIJAH: Elisha was asking God to fulfill His promise, imbuing him with His Spirit, as He had for Elijah. It was not a lack of faith that prompted these words, but a public declaration that all miracles were from the hand of the Lord and that he had been ordained as Elijah's successor.

16. LET THEM GO AND SEARCH: The sons of the prophets had not seen Elijah's miraculous, physical ascension into heaven, as Elisha had, so they naturally assumed that Elijah had died and left his body behind. If that had been the case, it would have been a disgraceful disrespect for the great prophet to leave his body unburied—but Elisha knew that Elijah had been taken to heaven without dying, so he told the others that their search would be futile.

17. THEY URGED HIM TILL HE WAS ASHAMED: That is, they wore him down with their importunate insistence. Elisha also knew that the search would prove to the prophets that Elijah had not died.

HEALING THE WATERS: *The school of prophets in Jericho has no drinkable water, but Elisha heals the brook.*

18. JERICHO: The Lord had destroyed the city of Jericho many years earlier, when the Israelites first entered the promised land under the leadership of Joshua. At that time, the Lord had pronounced a curse on the destroyed city, declaring that anyone who attempted to rebuild it would do so at the cost of his sons' lives (Joshua 6:26). This curse had been fulfilled just a few years prior to this event, when a man named Hiel attempted to rebuild Jericho and had lost two sons in the process (1 Kings 16:34).

20. A NEW BOWL . . . SALT: Here again we find Elisha calling for a clean vessel in which to work the Lord's miracle. The use of salt from a new jar symbolized the cleansing of the waters that God would miraculously do. The healing of Jericho's water, through Elisha, freed the city from Joshua's curse, making it habitable for humans once again.

21. NO MORE DEATH OR BARRENNESS: Only by God's will alone can death be eliminated and life be restored.

22. THE WATER REMAINS HEALED: Similarly, Christ's victory over death was absolute and final. When He establishes His eternal kingdom, there shall never again be any sin or death anywhere for all eternity.

⌇ READING 2 KINGS 6:8–23 ⌇

THE SYRIANS' SECRETS: *The king of Syria makes plans to attack Israel, but somehow his secrets keep making their way to the king of Israel.*

9. THE MAN OF GOD: That is, Elisha. The Lord gave him miraculous revelations concerning the Syrians' military plans, even though he was living in Israel, far to the south.

THE KING OF ISRAEL: Jehoram, the son of Ahab, was king in Israel at this time.

10. NOT JUST ONCE OR TWICE: That is, Elisha warned Jehoram numerous times of Syria's plans for invasion.

11. WHICH OF US IS FOR THE KING OF ISRAEL: The king of Syria was mystified as to how Jehoram continually anticipated his plans of attack. The only sensible answer, from a human perspective, was that he had a spy in his court.

12. ELISHA, THE PROPHET WHO IS IN ISRAEL: It is significant that Elisha's fame had spread into the Syrians' very court. (We will see another result of this in the next study.) Undoubtedly, word had spread of the miracles that the Lord worked through him, yet it is also true that the world takes note of those who stand faithfully for the Lord.

15. WHAT SHALL WE DO: The servant's consternation was quite understandable. Imagine his shock and dismay to step outside and discover that an enemy army had swept in silently during the night to surround his city in great force. There can be times in life when one is suddenly overwhelmed with suffering or circumstances beyond his control. But the servant did the right thing: he turned to the man of God for guidance.

16. DO NOT FEAR: Once again, we are reminded that fear is the enemy of God's people. The servant's initial response was a reflexive fear, but Elisha commanded him to put away that fear and rely instead on the power of God. Fear can cause a Christian to take rash and unwise actions, but turning the problem over to God in prayer will overcome the terror.

THOSE WHO ARE WITH US: Picture Elisha's servant looking around him with a puzzled expression at these words, wondering who on earth the prophet was referring to. But Elisha was not referring to any earthly power at all, but to the heavenly hosts that the servant's fleshly eyes could not see.

SPIRITUAL SIGHT, PHYSICAL BLINDNESS: *The Lord allows the servant to see His spiritual reality, and blinds the Syrians to the physical realm.*

17. OPEN HIS EYES THAT HE MAY SEE: Elisha asked the Lord to enable His servant's physical eyes to see the hidden spiritual world for a moment, so his faith might also be strengthened. This is the essence of faith: to believe firmly in that which one cannot see, simply relying on God's promises (Hebrews 11:1).

18. BLINDNESS: The Lord had opened the servant's eyes to see the invisible spiritual reality around him; now He closed the Syrians' eyes so they could not even see the physical world. Those who lack spiritual sight are no better than these Syrian soldiers, stumbling through life like blind men. Spiritual sight, however, can only come from faith in Jesus Christ.

21. SHALL I KILL THEM . . . ? SHALL I KILL THEM?: King Jehoram's eagerness is almost amusing. He would certainly have been within his rights from a military point of view to slaughter the soldiers, since they had invaded Israel in force. But the Lord intended to demonstrate His mercy and grace, even to the enemies of His people.

MY FATHER: By using this expression, which conveyed the respect a child had for his father, King Jehoram of Israel acknowledged the authority of Elisha.

22. SET FOOD AND WATER BEFORE THEM: The act of sparing the soldiers' lives demonstrated mercy, withholding the death or captivity that was due them as a defeated army. But the Lord had His people go beyond mercy, providing a great banquet for their enemies and sending them back home in peace—and this demonstrated God's grace.

⌁ FIRST IMPRESSIONS ⌁

1. *Why do you think Elijah instructed Elisha to stay behind while he traveled from city to city? Why were the servants all talking about Elijah's departure? Why did Elisha ask them to stop?*

2. *What did Elisha mean when he requested a double portion of Elijah's spirit? Why did he desire such a thing?*

3. *Read Joshua 6:26, followed by 1 Kings 16:34. What significance did Elisha's act have in regard to God's healing something that had once been subject to a curse?*

4.   *What did Elisha mean when he cried out, "My father, my father, the chariot of Israel and its horsemen" (2 Kings 2:12)?*

⌁ SOME KEY PRINCIPLES ⌁

The Lord will one day return to take His children home.

Elijah was one of only two men in the Bible who were taken to heaven without dying. His dramatic ascension in a whirlwind, accompanied by a chariot of fire and horses, demonstrated that God has absolute command over all the forces of nature, including death. It seemed utterly impossible to those left behind that a man might escape death, and the Scriptures tell us clearly that "it is appointed for men to die once" (Hebrews 9:27)—yet they searched diligently and found no body of Elijah, for there was none to find.

We are not told why God chose to do this for Elijah, yet part of His reason was to present a clear demonstration to His people that He is able to whisk them into His presence suddenly, in the twinkling of an eye. The Bible promises that this very thing will happen one day, when "the Lord Himself will descend from heaven with a shout, with the voice of an archangel, and with the trumpet of God. . . . Then we who are alive and remain shall be caught up . . . in the clouds to meet the Lord in the air. And thus we shall always be with the Lord" (1 Thessalonians 4:16–17).

Just as Elijah and Elisha lived as messengers of God and walked in faithfulness to Him, the apostle Paul stated that he would be rewarded with a crown of righteousness from the Lord. What's more, Paul said this crown will also be awarded to "all who have loved His appearing" (2 Timothy 4:8). For the person who walks in faithfulness to Jesus Christ, His return to earth to be with His people forever is a sight to be longed for and desired. Skeptics may doubt that the Lord can take someone from the earth miraculously and without experiencing death. But Elijah's departure is an encouragement for us to long for the Lord's coming.

God demonstrates both mercy and grace through Christ.

Elisha delivered the enemy Syrian army into the hand of King Jehoram, walking them right into the middle of his fortified capital city. This army had come in force against Israel, intending to fully overrun them once they had captured the prophet of God. King Jehoram, therefore, would have been fully justified in taking the men as slaves, or even in putting them to death. The one thing that no sensible king would have done in that situation would be to set the army free, allowing them to regroup and return in greater force at a later date.

Yet this is exactly what the Lord commanded King Jehoram to do: set the enemies free, and allow them to return to Syria in peace. This was God's demonstration of His mercy to the Syrians, showing these Gentiles that He is a merciful and forgiving God. This deed would have been remarkable enough by itself, but God's generosity did not stop there: He further commanded the king to give the enemy army a great banquet, treating them as honored guests rather than as captured and hostile soldiers. This was the grace of God in action.

Mercy is the withholding of judgment that is rightfully due, setting the captured soldiers free; but grace goes beyond mercy by giving gifts to those who only deserve death. Both of these great qualities are found in perfect fullness in Jesus Christ. All mankind is deserving of God's wrath and judgment, for all have sinned against Him, and sin must be paid for by blood (Romans 3:23; Hebrews 9:22). But God in His mercy grants full forgiveness by imputing our sins to His Son; we are set free, like the Syrian soldiers, because Jesus bore God's wrath in our place. And God in His grace goes beyond this wonderful gift of salvation by pouring out His unlimited blessings upon His people, even to the point of giving us the presence of His Holy Spirit. Truly, as Paul wrote, our God "is able to do exceedingly abundantly above all that we ask or think, according to the power that works in us" (Ephesians 3:20), and we enjoy all these blessings through His Son, Jesus Christ.

Our security does not lie in military might.

The Syrians boasted a very powerful military in Elisha's day. Israel's army was also significant, yet the Syrians did not hesitate to send a powerful force deep into Israel's heart, nearly to the gates of her capital city. Their chariots and trained soldiers were astoundingly quiet as they surrounded the city of Dothan, a considerable accomplishment in its own right, and in the morning that small town awoke with dread to discover their hopeless situation. Who could save them from such an overwhelming foe, who'd come upon them with such breathtaking suddenness and ferocity?

Elisha knew the answer to that question, and he was not the least bit troubled by the situation. He knew that the hope of God's people is His character, not any military weapon or scheme of man. He did not need to see the Lord's mighty army surrounding their enemies; he knew by faith, rather than by sight. By the end of that memorable day, both Israel and Syria had learned that a nation's security lies in God's power, not its own military might.

This principle is just as true today as it was several thousand years ago in Elisha's generation. God has not changed; He is as faithful to deliver His people now as He was in Old Testament times. David wrote, "Some trust in chariots, and some in horses; but we will remember the name of the LORD our God" (Psalm 20:7). God calls His people to place their faith completely in Him, not in any form of human government or military. Isaiah warned, "Woe to those who go down to Egypt for help, and rely on horses, who trust in chariots because they are many, and in horsemen because they are very strong, but who do not look to the Holy One of Israel, nor seek the LORD!" (Isaiah 31:1). Christians need to emulate Elisha, asking the Lord to open our spiritual eyes that we might see His mighty hand and be encouraged.

⌣ DIGGING DEEPER ⌣

5. *In what ways did Elijah's ascension to heaven picture the rapture of Christ's church? How did it differ from the coming rapture?*

6. *Why did God tell Elisha the secret plans of the Syrian king? What does this teach about His character? About His protection?*

7. Why did God command King Jehoram to feed the Syrian army and send them home? How did this affect the Israelites? How did it affect the Syrians?

8. Israel's king wanted to strike the Syrian army down. Would he have been justified in doing so? What do you learn about God's character toward His enemies from this account?

ᴧ Taking It Personally ᴧ

9. If Jesus returned tonight, what would He find you doing? How would you feel about His appearance? How should His imminent return affect your life this week?

10. How does the Lord command us to demonstrate both mercy and grace to others? To whom might He be calling you to show His grace this week?

7

NAAMAN AND GEHAZI

2 KINGS 5

↪ CHARACTERS' BACKGROUND ↩

In our last study, we saw how the Lord gave His people a miraculous victory by revealing Syria's secret plans to Elisha. In this study, however, we will discover that the Lord also gave victories to Syria—even victories against His own people, Israel. At first glance, this seems shocking, because it might not fit our own preconceived expectations of how God works. But it is important to recognize that the Lord's plans often contradict our expectations. He works in and through the lives of all men, even nonbelievers, to accomplish His own sovereign plans.

This issue of what people expect God to do compared to what God is actually doing is the very issue that surfaces repeatedly in this chapter. We will meet a man named Naaman, a great general and powerful friend of the king of Syria, who also happened to have leprosy, a disfiguring disease that one would expect would disqualify him from such high-profile service. We will also meet a lowly slave girl, a powerless young person who was taken from Israel and forced to live in a land of pagans. One might expect such a girl to wilt and dry up spiritually under such circumstances, but instead we will find the opposite to be true. And in contrast to this little slave girl, we will also meet Elisha's right-hand man, the servant who was being groomed to take up the prophet's mantle of leadership. We would expect such a man to act with wisdom and propriety, but unfortunately that expectation will also prove wrong.

This theme of human expectation and the sovereignty of God runs strong through this study, and the people we'll meet will demonstrate how such expectations can be dangerous. Ironically, it will be a Gentile general who will teach an Israelite the proper way to obey God, even when His commands are surprising.

↪ READING 2 KINGS 5:1–27 ↩

NAAMAN THE SYRIAN: *Naaman is a great man in Syria who is powerful, respected—and a leper.*

1. Naaman: Meaning "gracious." Nothing is known of this man outside of this chapter, but what we are told here is quite striking. The description of him as "great and honorable" indicates that he was probably renowned and powerful, and he maintained a reputation as being a man of good character.

by him the Lord had given victory to Syria: This statement is also rather striking. First, it reminds us that all victory comes only from the Lord, and demonstrates that this important principle applies to all people, whether or not they fear God or worship pagan idols. Second, there is a possibility that some of Naaman's military victories were against Israel, which might seem to be paradoxical. Why would the Lord grant a victory to His people's enemies, especially if that victory meant His people's defeat? In His sovereignty, the Lord is always at work drawing some men to a saving faith, while simultaneously strengthening and disciplining those who have already made that step of faith. Israel at this time was apostate, chasing after pagan gods and spurning the ways of the true God, and He was using the Syrians to urge them to return to Him. At the same time, He also blessed Naaman by bringing him into the knowledge of God.

a leper: Despite his great stature, Naaman suffered from leprosy, a form of debilitating skin disease. Lepers were generally treated as outcasts in Old Testament times, and it is a further proof of Naaman's great stature in Syria that his condition did not interfere with his high position at the king's court.

2. brought back captive a young girl from . . . Israel: From the vantage point of the young slave girl, being enslaved and led away to a foreign land was undoubtedly a terrible fate. Yet, contrary to expectation, the Lord had greater plans in mind. From an eternal perspective, her temporary suffering would become worthwhile, as the Lord used her to lead Naaman to a knowledge of Himself. The Lord would use Daniel in a similar way, when he was later taken into captivity just prior to the exile of God's people.

3. he would heal him of his leprosy: This unnamed girl evidently remained faithful to God despite her difficult circumstances. She was alone in a foreign land, and far removed from anyone who worshiped the Lord, but still, she demonstrated a strong faith in God's healing power and knew that He would heal her master if he asked God's prophet, even though Naaman was a Gentile and an enemy of Israel.

4. Thus and thus said the girl: Naaman may well have been desperate to find a cure for his leprosy, willing even to follow the advice of a lowly slave girl. Whatever his motivation, listening to her advice was his first step of faith. This also demonstrates how the Lord uses the faithful testimonies of His people, even from those the world deems insignificant.

5. TEN TALENTS OF SILVER: Naaman's gift was literally fit for a king, consisting of approximately 750 pounds of silver, 150 pounds of gold, and 10 complete outfits of kingly raiment. The gold alone was equivalent to the annual wages of more than 500 common laborers in that economy, more than $2,500,000 in today's economy.

7. AM I GOD: One can hardly blame King Jehoram for his response to the letter from the king of Syria. Note that the letter said that Naaman had arrived before Jehoram "that *you* may heal him of his leprosy," as though the Syrians expected Jehoram to perform the miracle. It was not far-fetched for Jehoram to think that the Syrians were inventing some impossible task in order to have an excuse for open war. Nevertheless, Jehoram's response also betrayed a lack of faith in God's willingness to answer prayer. He correctly noted that only God can "kill and make alive," but he showed no inclination to *ask* God for Naaman's healing.

8. HE SHALL KNOW THAT THERE IS A PROPHET IN ISRAEL: Elisha recognized the golden opportunity that the king had missed, the chance to show the surrounding nations that the God of Israel was the one true God. Even from a political perspective, healing a Syrian could only be good for relations between Syria and Israel. But from an eternal perspective, Elisha knew that this opportunity might well bring a soul into relationship with God. Elisha understood well that one soul is worth more than all the gold in the world.

9. HE STOOD AT THE DOOR OF ELISHA'S HOUSE: Naaman's failing appears to have been vanity. He was accustomed to being treated with great deference and probably felt that the prophet was his social inferior.

10. ELISHA SENT A MESSENGER: This messenger was probably Gehazi, Elisha's servant. You will remember that Elisha used him as an intermediary with the woman from Shunem (Study 2). It appears that this was his way of mentoring Gehazi, as Elijah had mentored him.

ELISHA'S PRESCRIPTION: *Elisha tells Naaman to dip himself seven times in the Jordan. This is not what the great man expected.*

WASH IN THE JORDAN SEVEN TIMES: Elisha's instructions were designed to demonstrate clearly to Naaman that his healing was from God alone, not from some mystical power.

11. NAAMAN BECAME FURIOUS: Naaman's anger had several causes. First, he had been treated (as he saw it) with contempt by a social inferior, as the prophet would not even trouble himself to come out and speak with him—and this after being received properly at the court of Israel's king. Second, he probably thought that Elisha was instructing him on how to become ritually cleansed, without actually healing the leprosy. Bathing was an integral part of ritual cleansing, both in Israel and in the pagan nations, but Naaman wanted to be healed of his physical ailment, not of his spiritual condition. Elisha, however, was seeking to accomplish both.

WAVE HIS HAND: Naaman's expectations were somewhat amusing, and they also indicated his pagan background. He evidently expected Elisha to come forth and wave his hand over the leprosy and he'd be healed. He still had no knowledge of the omnipotent God of creation.

13. MY FATHER: It was not normal for servants to address their master in this way; it was more fitting in a mentoring relationship, such as Elisha had with Elijah. This indicates once again the sort of man Naaman was; even his servants viewed him as a father figure. Indeed, their intercession here indicated that they sincerely wanted to see him healed.

IF THE PROPHET HAD TOLD YOU TO DO SOMETHING GREAT: These servants demonstrated keen insight and wisdom in this advice. Naaman was clearly prepared to do anything, regardless of the difficulty, in order to be healed of his leprosy, and it was all the better that the required action was so easy. Yet this principle also applies on a larger scale to our fallen human nature, which often leads men to think that they can atone for their own sins by performing some great spiritual feat or costly penance. The true means of salvation, however, is found in confessing one's sins, asking forgiveness, and trusting in Christ's sacrifice as one's Lord. It is the very simplicity of this message that often causes sinners to reject God's offer.

A SOUL IS SAVED: *Naaman sees that the Lord is the one true God, and believes with all his heart.*

15. NOW I KNOW THAT THERE IS NO GOD IN ALL THE EARTH, EXCEPT IN ISRAEL: Naaman went to Israel to find healing for his physical disease, but he left both physically *and* spiritually healed. His statement is a clear declaration of faith in God, and it also puts to shame a great portion of Israel, the very people who were supposed to be a testimony to the world around them of the power and presence of the one true God. Instead, they tried to worship both God and Baal (1 Kings 18).

16. I WILL RECEIVE NOTHING: Elisha rejected Naaman's gift because he wanted it to be absolutely clear that he was in no way responsible for Naaman's healing. Elisha did accept gifts at other times, including the hospitality of the woman from Shunem, but such gifts were intended to support the ministry of a man of God, meeting his daily needs. Naaman's gift was intended as payment for services rendered, and God's people are never to seek profit from God's grace. (See Acts 8 for another example.) As we shall see, Gehazi did not understand this principle.

18. MAY THE LORD PARDON YOUR SERVANT: Naaman also anticipated a difficulty when he returned home to Syria, since he apparently was required in his job to accompany the king to pagan worship ceremonies. He could not see any way around that difficulty, not yet understanding that the God who healed his incurable disease could also resolve his difficult circumstances.

19. GO IN PEACE: Elisha's response to Naaman demonstrates God's patience and mercy. The Lord wants His people to grow in their knowledge of His character and His Word, but He is not a harsh taskmaster; He does not demand that a new convert grow into spiritual maturity overnight.

GEHAZI'S GREED: *Elisha's servant is overwhelmed with the greatness of Naaman's gift, and yields to deadly temptation.*

20. MY MASTER HAS SPARED NAAMAN THIS SYRIAN: Elisha's servant, Gehazi, revealed some degree of resentment and national prejudice in these words. He seemed to resent Naaman's healing, preferring to see him perish, but his hostility had clouded his thinking. He should have rejoiced in Naaman's conversion, rather than wishing him ill simply because he was "this Syrian."

22. MY MASTER HAS SENT ME: One sin leads to another, as we have seen in previous studies. In this case, Gehazi's covetousness led to telling lies. Yet Gehazi's lie was even more insidious because it impugned not only Elisha's character but God's as well. Naaman was a new believer, and his understanding of God's ways was incomplete—and here was the servant of God's spokesman saying that God's prophets did, in fact, accept payment for their services. Gehazi was doing more than grasping profit for himself; he was also stealing from God's glory.

23. TWO TALENTS OF SILVER: That is, approximately 150 pounds of silver. In today's economy, this would be worth more than $40,000; it was more than five years' salary for the common laborer in the economy of that time.

THEY CARRIED THEM ON AHEAD OF HIM: It is true that it would have been difficult for Gehazi to carry 150 pounds of silver by himself, but having a servant running ahead indicated that a man was important in some way. Gehazi was indulging his desire for recognition and human praise, as well as for wealth. Both are simply forms of covetousness, and both can still be snares for Christians today.

24. STORED THEM AWAY IN THE HOUSE: Gehazi's sin is reminiscent of the sin of Achan, who tried to hide stolen loot by burying it under his tent—which cost the lives of Achan and his whole family. (See Joshua 7.)

25. YOUR SERVANT DID NOT GO ANYWHERE: Yet another sin was added to the list: Gehazi also lied to Elisha.

26. DID NOT MY HEART GO WITH YOU: The Lord had revealed Gehazi's actions to Elisha, and he knew the truth even before he asked Gehazi where he had gone—in fact, in asking him that question, Elisha was offering him a chance to confess his sin and repent. His use of the word "heart," rather than "mind," suggests the affection that he had for his servant. Elisha probably had great hopes for Gehazi to take up his mantle one day, just as he had done for Elijah, but on this sad day those hopes died.

✌ FIRST IMPRESSIONS ✌

1. *Why did Elisha instruct Naaman to wash seven times in the Jordan? Why did Naaman become so angry? What would have happened if he had refused to do so? What did he gain by obeying?*

2. *What motivated Gehazi to take the gift from Naaman? Why did this action bring leprosy upon him? What harm did his actions cause to others besides himself?*

3. *How did Naaman's character compare with Gehazi's? What were the priorities of each man's life? How did each respond to God's commands?*

4. How did Gehazi's attitude toward Naaman compare with that of Naaman's slave girl? How did each of them view the unbelieving Gentiles?

↶ Some Key Principles ↷

God pours out His blessings on those who believe in Him.

The Syrians were Gentiles, not members of God's chosen people, the descendants of Abraham. What's worse, they were Israel's powerful enemy, engaged in long-standing border raids, frequently carrying Israelites away into slavery. Naaman himself was a powerful and successful general, and probably was responsible (from a human standpoint) for Syria's victories over the Lord's people. Yet when he asked God's prophet for healing of an incurable disease, the Lord honored his faith and his request.

The reason for God's grace in healing Naaman was that the Lord is eager to pour out His blessings on those who exercise faith in Him, regardless of that person's background or upbringing. Indeed, the Lord had been the one who gave Naaman his great victories and successes, even against God's own people. The Lord did this to bless Naaman and move him toward a faith in Himself, but He also gave Naaman success in order to move the people of Israel back into obedience to His Word. The sad truth is that the Lord wanted to pour out His blessings on Israel as well, but His people refused to ask. A Gentile had exercised more faith than the people of God were willing to show.

Jesus addressed this very issue when He spoke of the fact that a prophet is not honored among his own people. There were many widows in Israel during the great famine of Elijah's time, He told his listeners, but God's prophet went to none of them; instead, he went to a Gentile widow. There were also many lepers in Israel during Elisha's time, but God's prophet healed none of them—only Naaman the Syrian was healed (Luke 4:24–27). God wanted to help them all, but the Gentiles were the only ones who asked for His help; God's own people turned instead to Baal. Today, as then, the Lord wants to help one and all—but He does require that we trust Him.

The Lord calls us to obey Him, even if His commands don't meet our expectations.

Naaman was a great and powerful leader in one of the world's mightiest nations, and he was accustomed to being treated with deference. He was a general in the army, and his soldiers saluted him and obeyed his orders. He was a wealthy and influential man in the king's court, and his peers addressed him with respect, but when he arrived at the door of a lowly prophet, a foreign seer who had no wealth or pomp, he found himself standing outside and being addressed by the prophet's servant. This was not what he expected.

He had traveled to Israel to find a man of great power who could heal him of his incurable leprosy. Elisha did not act as Naaman expected, but instead, he told Naaman to go away and bathe in a muddy river, indicating that the prophet was not even the one who would heal him. The entire experience was quite shocking to Naaman, because nothing fit his expectations.

Nevertheless, Naaman obeyed the command of God, and his skin was miraculously healed. More important, his soul was saved and his spiritual eyes were opened to an understanding of the God of Israel. Naaman had to let go of his own expectations and desires, submitting himself to obey God's commands, given through His prophet, even though they didn't make any sense to him at the time. God's ways are not our ways, and we cannot comprehend all of God's sovereign purposes and designs. There are times when He commands us to do things that are contrary to our culture's teachings, to what everyone else is doing, and to everything that we would expect. At such times, we must remember that God's ways are always right, regardless of what the world may tell us, and we can only follow Him by obeying His ways.

The sin of covetousness can destroy a person's ministry.

Gehazi had a unique ministry, being privileged to work beside Elisha. He assisted the prophet in performing great miracles of the Lord's power, and he was blessed with hearing the Word of God, day in and day out, right from the mouth of God's chief spokesman in Israel. He probably also had a great ministry ahead of him, as he evidently was being trained by Elisha to take on the mantle of prophetic leadership when the time came. These things indicate that he was a godly man, qualified for such a ministry as few others would have been. He undoubtedly had some rough edges, as we all do, but the Lord was at work to smooth those rough spots and equip him for greater areas of service.

Gehazi was dazzled by the immense wealth of Naaman's gift, enough gold and silver to live in comfort and ease for the rest of his days. He also evidently coveted honor and prestige, as he walked behind two servants, who carried his newfound loot, like a triumphant warrior returning from battle. Perhaps Gehazi justified such indulgences in his own mind by telling himself how he would use the wealth and honor to further the Lord's work; but even such excuses do not justify greed. The truth is that he had "cashed in" on God's grace, using God's work of salvation for his own material gain—and this sin resulted in permanent damage to his own ministry.

Gehazi's sin did not end his walk with God, for he appeared later still serving Elisha, but it did damage his testimony and severely hinder his future effectiveness in ministry. This principle holds true for any area of sin, not just covetousness. The Lord does not abandon His children when they indulge in sinful behavior, but such disobedience may permanently disqualify us from future areas of service. The Bible instructs us on how to avoid the tragedy of Gehazi: "Do not love the world or the things in the world. If anyone loves the world, the love of the Father is not in him. For all that is in the world—the lust of the flesh, the lust of the eyes, and the pride of life—is not of the Father but is of the world. And the world is passing away, and the lust of it; but he who does the will of God abides forever" (1 John 2:15–17).

⌁ DIGGING DEEPER ⌁

5. Why did God choose to heal Naaman, even though he was an unbeliever and a Gentile? Why did God give him military victories over His own people?

6. In what ways were both Naaman and Gehazi shocked by Elisha's words? How did each man respond to God's unexpected instructions? How did the actions of an unsaved Gentile add shame to one of God's people?

7. In your own words, define the following sins, and provide practical examples of each.
Lust of the flesh:

Lust of the eyes:

Pride of life:

8. When has God's Word called you to something that surprised you? How did His commands contradict your expectations? How did you respond?

⤳ Taking It Personally ⤲

9. Are you struggling with some sin that might threaten your testimony for the Lord? How will you follow the example of Naaman, rather than Gehazi?

10. How do you tend to treat non-Christians? How can you direct them toward faith in Christ?

8

JEHOIADA THE HIGH PRIEST

⤳ CHARACTER'S BACKGROUND ⤶

Jehoshaphat's son, Jehoram, became king in Judah after his father's death, but he did not follow his father's example. He murdered his brothers when he ascended the throne in order to prevent them from trying to take it from him, and he then proceeded to lead Judah into absolute paganism. As if this were not enough, he also married the daughter of Israel's king Ahab and queen Jezebel, the most evil of all Israel's rulers. Over the years, this woman would cause trouble for Judah just as her mother had for Israel. The writer of 2 Chronicles poignantly summarized Jehoram's reign: "He was thirty-two years old when he became king. He reigned in Jerusalem eight years and, to no one's sorrow, departed" (21:20).

Jehoram's son Ahaziah took the throne after his father's death, but he only reigned for one year. Upon his death, his mother, Athaliah, seized her opportunity to take the throne of Judah, and she set about murdering all her grandchildren so that there would be no one left who could displace her by claiming the throne. Fortunately, there were still godly people left in Judah, including the high priest Jehoiada and his wife, Jehoshabeath. This godly couple rescued Joash, one of Ahaziah's sons, and hid him in the temple. Over the next six years, Jehoiada instructed young Joash in the ways of the Lord, training him to become a godly king who would break the wickedness perpetrated by both his father and grandfather, and return the nation to the fear of the Lord. Once Joash finally ascended the throne, Jehoiada continued to act as his counselor and mentor, and during those years Joash led the people of Judah in righteousness.

⤳ READING 2 CHRONICLES 24:1–22 ⤶

JUDAH'S BOY KING: *Young Joash is only seven years old when he becomes king, and he is guided by Jehoiada the high priest.*

1. JOASH: The great-grandson of King Jehoshaphat. He became king around 835 BC. Jehoiada's wife, Jehoshabeath, was his aunt.

2. ALL THE DAYS OF JEHOIADA THE PRIEST: Joash had been raised in the temple by Jehoiada the high priest and had been instructed by his godly protector in God's ways and Law. He became king when he was only seven years old, so it is very likely that Jehoiada also acted as one of his chief advisors for many years, strongly influencing his reign. Things would change, however, after the high priest's death.

3. JEHOIADA TOOK TWO WIVES FOR HIM: The Lord had commanded His people to not take multiple wives (Deuteronomy 17:17), so it seems strange that the high priest would have the king take two wives. This may be an indication that the Lord's commands were gradually being forgotten at this time; we will look more closely at this topic in Study 10. Nevertheless, Jehoiada was trying to help Joash build a godly family, and he took a strong interest in ensuring that the king married Israelite women rather than Canaanites, as many other kings before Joash had done, including Solomon.

REPAIRING THE TEMPLE: *Joash sets his heart on repairing the Lord's temple in Jerusalem, but not everyone shares his zeal.*

4. JOASH SET HIS HEART: At this point in his reign, Joash was being influenced by Jehoiada's godly counsel, and he fully embraced that godly counsel, following the priorities of God. The fact that he set his heart on repairing the temple indicated that his heart was turned toward God at this time, and he desired to do the things that would please the Lord. This was probably a direct result of Jehoiada's faithful mentoring.

5. THE LEVITES DID NOT DO IT QUICKLY: Joash had made it clear that the temple repairs were a high priority in his mind, as they were in the Lord's mind, but the priests (Levites) did not comply. We are not told why they failed to repair the temple, but the author's tone suggests that they did not share the king's desire to renew the Lord's house of worship. Apparently, Jehoiada did not instill in his fellow Levites the same heart for God that he had taught to the king.

7. THE SONS OF ATHALIAH: Joash's grandmother Athaliah had worshiped Baal, like her mother, Jezebel, and during her tenure her sons had broken into the temple and stolen many of the sacred treasures, to dedicate them to their false god. However, even the parallel account of this in 2 Kings 12 states that the temple was in a state of "dilapidation" (v. 5), suggesting that the temple had been allowed to fall into disrepair over a long period of time. This demonstrates that the syncretism that was plaguing both Israel and Judah had led the people to all but abandon the proper form of worship to the Lord, which was to take place only at the temple in Jerusalem.

TAKING A COLLECTION: *Joash asks the people of Judah to help financially, and the response is overwhelming.*

9. THE COLLECTION THAT MOSES . . . HAD IMPOSED: See Exodus 30:12–16.

10. ALL THE LEADERS AND ALL THE PEOPLE REJOICED: Some of the monetary contributions were prescribed by the Mosaic law, but the use of the chest also permitted free-will offerings. The people of Judah evidently were very eager to participate in the temple's renewal, and much of the cost was apparently funded through voluntary giving—"until all had given." What is particularly striking about this offering is that the money was given with a spirit of rejoicing. There was evidently no begrudging the contributions, as all the people eagerly took part in restoring the Lord's place of worship.

11. GATHERED MONEY IN ABUNDANCE: This again demonstrated the willing hearts of the people of Judah, who gave so cheerfully that more than enough was collected for the work at hand.

13. SO THE WORKMEN LABORED: Everyone in Judah participated in this great renewal project, some using the skills the Lord had given them to do the work, others providing the finances needed to carry it out. The 2 Kings account adds that "they did not require an account from the men into whose hand they delivered the money to be paid to workmen, for they dealt faithfully" (12:15).

14–15. THEY OFFERED BURNT OFFERINGS . . . ALL THE DAYS OF JEHOIADA. BUT: The word *but* brings the reader up short in these verses, indicating that there was about to be an abrupt change once Jehoiada left the scene. As long as he was involved in the king's life, the people worshiped the Lord continually but, after his death, things would begin to deteriorate once again.

THE DEATH OF JEHOIADA: *The high priest dies, leaving the king without a counselor. Joash walks on his own.*

16. THEY BURIED HIM . . . AMONG THE KINGS: This was a very high honor, as no other high priest is recorded to have been buried among the kings. It indicates that the people of Judah recognized the godly influence that Jehoiada had exercised on the reign of their king. They apparently ascribed to him the spiritual renewal that had taken place. Subsequent events would demonstrate that this was indeed the case.

17. THE KING LISTENED TO THEM: It appears that Joash had never learned how to take the principles taught by his mentor and begin to apply them for himself. He had evidently relied very heavily on Jehoiada's counsel, and when the high priest was no longer available, he began to turn to others for guidance. It is quite significant that these counselors were the leaders of Judah, not just some random friends. The previous suppression of these leaders is an indication of the strong leadership that Jehoiada had exercised during his time as high priest, since evidently the political leaders were opposed to his determination to restore correct worship practices in Judah.

18. THEY LEFT THE HOUSE OF THE LORD GOD: The people of Israel and Judah had added pagan practices into their worship ceremony for so long that it seemed like a newfangled idea when they were called to return to obedience to what God had actually commanded to their ancestors. Judah's leadership may well have considered Jehoiada a sort of fanatic who insisted on old-fashioned and outdated worship. Once he was out of the way, they could relax and "not take things so seriously." In other words, they could go back to inventing their own worship practices and disregarding God's Word and His prescribed ways.

WRATH CAME UPON JUDAH: Men may not take God's worship seriously, but the Lord does. He has given believers clear instructions on how to serve Him and worship Him, and He expects His people to obey them.

19. HE SENT PROPHETS TO THEM: Once again we see the Lord's patience and long-suffering toward His people's persistent disobedience. Their wickedness stirred up His wrath, yet He stayed His hand in mercy, and extended the grace of continuing to send them prophets to lead them back into obedience.

21. STONED HIM WITH STONES IN THE COURT OF THE HOUSE OF THE LORD: The wicked leaders of Judah defiled the temple court, so courageously cleansed and renewed under Jehoiada, by murdering Jehoiada's own son in that place under the express command of Joash, whose life had been so blessed by Jehoiada. Joash's reign began well but ended with the darkest disgrace. His treachery was later repaid when his own servants conspired to murder him.

⌁ FIRST IMPRESSIONS ⌁

1. *Why did Jehoiada and his wife take such great risks to save Joash's life? What was the result of their selfless acts?*

2. Why did Joash set his heart on rebuilding the temple? How had the temple fallen into disrepair? Why did the priests not obey the king's commands?

3. What motivated the people of Judah to give so generously to the rebuilding project? How does their example apply to God's people today?

4. Why did Joash forget what he owed Jehoiada's family? Why did he have Jehoiada's son murdered? What should he have done instead?

ᕔ Some Key Principles ᕔ

Train the next generation to faithfully serve the Lord.

We have seen many mentors in the course of these studies. Elijah trained Elisha; Elisha trained Gehazi; Jehoiada trained Joash. Some of these mentoring relationships were more effective than others, but they all have a few things in common. First, there was always a close relationship between mentor and pupil. In these examples, the men actually lived together and spent most of their waking hours working together. Second, the mentor's training included both practical experience and theoretical teaching. Elisha had Gehazi get involved interacting with other people, giving him opportunities to develop interpersonal skills as well as a heart for the needs of others, while Jehoiada set Joash on the throne of Judah, where he took on the affairs of overseeing a nation.

One critical step in mentoring is illustrated by these various relationships, and that is the mentor's need to train his pupil to rely on God rather than on human counselors. Elisha learned this important lesson, and it enabled him to take over his mentor's responsibilities once Elijah's ministry was completed. Joash did not learn this critical lesson, and it destroyed what had begun as a godly career as king. Apparently, Joash never went beyond relying on Jehoiada for direction and counsel. He never learned how to serve the Lord and rely upon His Word. This step is vital, as illustrated in Joash's life, because it is at the core of Christian mentorship. Teaching others to be faithful servants requires teaching them how to draw close to God themselves.

The process of mentoring was invented by God, and His original structure for the process is the immediate family. It is no coincidence in Scripture that the disciple frequently refers to his mentor as "father," for God intended human fathers to be loving mentors to their entire families. He commanded His people, "These words which I command you today shall be in your heart. You shall teach them diligently to your children, and shall talk of them when you sit in your house, when you walk by the way, when you lie down, and when you rise up" (Deuteronomy 6:6–7). Notice the process He specified: keep His Word in your heart; teach diligently; talk about God's Word during all daily activities. This presupposes two things: the mentor will be diligently studying God's Word on his own; and also that he will be spending most of his waking hours with his pupils—in this case his children—including them in his day-to-day activities. When God's people follow this pattern, they effectively train the next generation to walk in the ways of the Lord, and also teach them by example to do the same for their own children.

Avoid the sin of ingratitude.

King Joash owed a great deal to the spiritual leadership and friendship of Jehoiada—indeed, he owed his very life to the high priest and his wife. Their act of preserving him from his grandmother's deadly plot was performed at great risk to themselves, for Athaliah would not have hesitated to kill them if she had caught them. Yet Jehoiada's gifts did not end with the preservation of Joash's life; the high priest undoubtedly taught the young boy from the Word of God during the years when he was living at the temple. He later gathered the people together and made Joash king, again at great risk to himself, and then continued to counsel him in the ways of righteousness.

But Joash forgot all these things; he "did not remember the kindness which Jehoiada his father had done to him" (2 Chronicles 24:22), and that same forgetfulness led him directly into a very great sin. How could a man forget such costly and selfless love, especially when he owed his kingship and his life to the man who'd been like a father to him? The answer to that question is found in the heart of every human being. We are all prone to commit the sin of ingratitude, just as we are prone to disobey God's commands. Joash fell into ingratitude because he forgot to remember the goodness God had shown to him through the life of Jehoida. When we fail to remember the goodness of God toward us, the result threatens us all.

Gratitude requires a person to remember the blessings he has received through the efforts of another, and that remembering requires deliberate effort. This is the reason the Scriptures command us to deliberately remember all the Lord has done on our behalf, for without such deliberate recollection, we will quickly take His love and kindness for granted and fall prey to the sin of ingratitude. "Bless the LORD, O my soul," wrote the great ancestor of Joash, King David, "and forget not all His benefits" (Psalm 103:2). This is done by choosing to rejoice rather than complain, by intentionally focusing on a spirit of thankfulness, and by taking our gratitude directly to God. Paul wrote, "Rejoice always, pray without ceasing, in everything give thanks; for this is the will of God in Christ Jesus for you" (1 Thessalonians 5:16–18).

The Lord loves a cheerful giver.

King Joash commanded the Levites to oversee repairs to the temple in Jerusalem, a very important priority for God's people—but they did not obey. They did not rebel openly; they simply didn't make it a priority because they lacked any zeal for the project. So Joash placed a "donations chest" outside the temple, and called upon the people of Judah to donate voluntarily—and the people responded with the zeal that the priests lacked. In fact, their gifts amounted to more than what was required, as they poured out their contributions with an open hand.

This generosity actually grows out of a spirit of gratitude, which we discussed in the last section. When we remember to be grateful for all the Lord has done, we naturally respond by wanting to give to Him, and it is that very spirit of eagerness that delights the heart of God. The opposite of this is also true: when we have a begrudging spirit toward the Lord, it is probably growing out of a spirit of ingratitude. What's more, the one feeds the other—a spirit of gratitude prompts us to give generously; when we give generously, the Lord blesses generously, giving us yet more for which to be grateful.

The Lord is not a hard taskmaster, and He does not demand a heavy tax burden from His people. Indeed, the opportunity to give to His work on earth is yet another of His blessings, for it allows each of us to take part in His work to people throughout the earth. And when we give generously, He has promised to give us even greater blessings— which in turn will enable us to continue giving generously. Paul taught, "He who sows sparingly will also reap sparingly, and he who sows bountifully will also reap bountifully. So let each one give as he purposes in his heart, not grudgingly or of necessity; for God loves a cheerful giver" (2 Corinthians 9:6–7).

ᕈ Digging Deeper ᕈ

5. Why did Judah revert to paganism so quickly after Jehoiada's death? What does this suggest about the spiritual condition of the priests at the time?

6. What practical lessons can you glean from the various mentors in these studies? Consider Elijah/Elisha, Elisha/Gehazi, Jehoiada/Joash, and others.

7. What sin is at the root of an ungrateful spirit? How can a Christian cultivate a generous spirit? Why is this important?

8. Who has been a mentor in your life? Who might list you as a mentor in their own lives? Who might the Lord want you to mentor in the future?

ᑐ Taking It Personally ᑕ

9. Do you tend to give cheerfully or begrudgingly? How can you cultivate a generous spirit in the future?

10. List below ten things that you are thankful for; then spend time in prayer thanking the Lord for His countless blessings in your life.

THE MINISTRY OF ELISHA

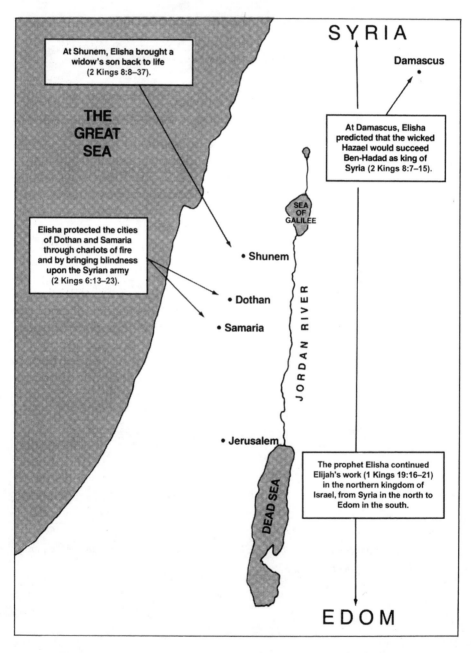

At Shunem, Elisha brought a widow's son back to life (2 Kings 8:8–37).

THE GREAT SEA

At Damascus, Elisha predicted that the wicked Hazael would succeed Ben-Hadad as king of Syria (2 Kings 8:7–15).

Elisha protected the cities of Dothan and Samaria through chariots of fire and by bringing blindness upon the Syrian army (2 Kings 6:13–23).

SYRIA

Damascus

SEA OF GALILEE

• Shunem

• Dothan

JORDAN RIVER

• Samaria

• Jerusalem

DEAD SEA

The prophet Elisha continued Elijah's work (1 Kings 19:16–21) in the northern kingdom of Israel, from Syria in the north to Edom in the south.

EDOM

~ 9 ~
HEZEKIAH

↪ CHARACTER'S BACKGROUND ↩

Hezekiah's father was King Ahaz, a man who did not obey the Lord's commands but led the people of Judah into wickedness. Unlike his father, Hezekiah broke that pattern and turned his heart toward the Lord. Scripture tells us that Judah never had a king like Hezekiah either before or after his time (2 Kings 18:7). He walked in the ways of the Lord, and even went farther in righteousness than other good kings by tearing down the high places that had plagued both Israel and Judah for generations.

In the history of the Israelites, God would often bless obedience with times of peace and prosperity for the land and people. Yet God, in His sovereignty, had a different plan for Hezekiah and his reign. Despite Judah having the godliest king in centuries, in the fourth year of Hezekiah's reign, the nation of Israel was attacked by Assyria and eventually taken into captivity. Eight years later, Assyria attacked Judah as well, intending to do with them as they had done with Israel and many other nations. This difficult situation illustrates the fact that the Lord does often permit His people to face trials and hardship. Such situations do not necessarily indicate that the Lord is angry with His people; there are times when He chooses to use difficult circumstances to increase our faith and grow us in blessings.

This was the case with Hezekiah, who faced one of the most dangerous times in Judah's history. The nation's fate hung in the balance, but King Hezekiah knew how to respond: he took the burden to the Lord, and trusted Him to fight the battle.

↪ READING 2 KINGS 18:13–37 ↩

THE ASSYRIAN THREAT: *Sennacherib, king of the Assyrians, demands an outrageous tribute from Judah.*

13. THE FOURTEENTH YEAR OF KING HEZEKIAH: Hezekiah ruled in Judah from approximately 715 to 686 BC. In the sixth year of his reign, Assyria had besieged Samaria and taken the people of Israel into captivity. Now, eight years later, the Assyrians turned their attention to the destruction of Judah as well.

14. I HAVE DONE WRONG: Hezekiah's father, King Ahaz, had submitted to Assyria's tyranny, agreeing to pay tribute to its pagan king. This was not the Lord's will for His people, as He had commanded the Israelites to make no covenants with the Gentile nations (Deuteronomy 7:2). When Hezekiah first took the throne, he boldly threw off the yoke of servitude to Assyria that his father had established. Unfortunately, even Hezekiah gave in under the pressure of the Assyrian army and tried to rectify the situation by paying tribute.

WHATEVER YOU IMPOSE ON ME I WILL PAY: Sennacherib asked for about eleven tons of silver and one ton of gold. In order to pay this, Hezekiah emptied the temple and palace treasuries and stripped the layers of gold off the doors and doorposts of the temple. This was a sad day for Judah and Hezekiah's reign. Unfortunately, despite Hezekiah's efforts, Sennacherib still demanded Judah's surrender.

TAUNTS AND BOASTS: *Messengers from Assyria stand outside Judah's walls and try to sow discord and fear.*

17. THE TARTAN, THE RABSARIS, AND THE RABSHAKEH: These were titles for the general of the Assyrian army, a high-ranking court official, and a field commander, respectively.

19. WHAT CONFIDENCE IS THIS IN WHICH YOU TRUST: The Rabshakeh essentially meant, "Just who do you think you are, rebelling against Assyria?" Yet his words suggest that Hezekiah's rebellion against Assyria was seen by the Gentiles as an open declaration that he had faith in his God. The Assyrians took this as an affront to *their* gods, as Hezekiah was effectively saying that his God was greater than theirs.

22. HE WHOSE HIGH PLACES AND WHOSE ALTARS HEZEKIAH HAS TAKEN AWAY: The irony of this statement is that it was *not* the Lord's altars that were removed from the high places, but the very syncretistic shrines that we have encountered throughout these studies. The Rabshakeh's speech was an early example of enemy propaganda during wartime, designed to cause division and strife within Judah.

23. IF YOU ARE ABLE ... TO PUT RIDERS ON THEM: The Assyrian turned his taunts from Judah's God to Judah's military, pointing out that she lacked both weapons and the men to wield them. It is unlikely that Judah had any chariot forces, and the Israelites as a whole generally fought on foot rather than on horseback. Assyria's military might was vastly superior to Judah's—but King Hezekiah knew better than to rely on anything other than God.

25. THE LORD SAID TO ME: The Assyrian speaker concluded his masterpiece of propaganda by referring to the prophecies of Isaiah, in which the Lord had warned His people that He would send the Assyrians against them (Isaiah 8:7–8). The Rabshakeh was essentially telling the people of Judah that his army was there to fulfill that prophecy, and his words undoubtedly struck fear in the hearts of God's people.

26. DO NOT SPEAK TO US IN HEBREW: Aramaic was spoken by educated people throughout Canaan in that day, while Hebrew was the language of the Jews. The Assyrians chose to speak in Hebrew rather than Aramaic for that very reason: they wanted the Jews to understand their words, in hopes of creating fear and insurrection within Judah. This is the tactic the devil uses, even today, always working to cause division and strife among God's people.

29. DO NOT LET HEZEKIAH DECEIVE YOU: This taunt inadvertently gave high praise to King Hezekiah, as it demonstrated that his commitment to the Lord was known even in the pagan world, and it also showed that he urged his people to trust in the Lord.

32. THE LORD WILL DELIVER US: In this masterpiece of twisted logic, the Assyrians claimed that they were coming as God's tool of judgment upon His people, while simultaneously urging the people to not trust in Him. The devil loves to twist God's Word, sowing confusion among God's people if possible. It is always important that Christians know how to rightly divide the word of truth (2 Timothy 2:15).

36. THE PEOPLE HELD THEIR PEACE: This statement demonstrates the effective leadership of King Hezekiah, for the people remained silent out of obedience to his command. It is also a good example of how to respond to the devil's arguments, for there are times when the best response is no response.

⤳ READING 2 KINGS 19:1–37 ⤳

HEZEKIAH'S RESPONSE: *Rather than arguing with the Assyrians, Hezekiah turns to the Lord for an answer.*

1. HEZEKIAH . . . WENT INTO THE HOUSE OF THE LORD: The people were commanded to not respond to the Assyrians' defiance, but the king did respond—by going before the Lord.

3. TROUBLE, AND REBUKE, AND BLASPHEMY: Hezekiah enumerated three sources of evil in this phrase. The people were facing trouble, which refers to any problem caused by an external source, but they were also facing the Lord's deliberate rebuke of His people.

In this, Hezekiah acknowledged that the Lord had just cause against the people of Judah for their many years of unfaithfulness. But the third source of evil was Rabshakeh's blasphemous words, urging God's people to remove their faith from God and place it in the strength and kindly intentions of the Assyrians. Hezekiah called upon the Lord to turn His rebuke against the Assyrians for their blasphemy against His name.

6. Do not be afraid: Once again, the Lord commanded His people to not yield to fear. The Assyrians were counting on the people's fear to drive them directly into their hands, just as the devil uses fear to drive people into his nets of destruction.

Hezekiah's Prayer: *The king takes Sennacherib's defiant words and spreads them before the Lord.*

10. Do not let your God . . . deceive you: Sennacherib had previously accused Hezekiah of deceiving the people of Judah concerning God's intentions and abilities, but here he went to the heart of his real accusation by accusing God of being a deceiver. This blasphemy was at least as wicked as the previous one, since it essentially accused God, the Source of truth, of being the devil, who is the father of lies.

14. Spread it before the Lord: Hezekiah's act is a perfect picture of how God's people should deal with overwhelming threats, as he lay his difficulty out before the Lord. He was effectively saying, "Here is the letter I received, Lord. Please save us from this situation."

15. You have made heaven and earth: Hezekiah expressed a fundamental truth: He who created the earth is also God of the earth. The world has always tried to deny this truth, as it does today with the false religion of evolution, but it is an inescapable fact. There is only one God of the entire universe, and He rules it, because He alone created it.

16. The living God: Hezekiah also touched upon another fundamental truth: the Lord is the only living God; all the other gods men serve are mere fictions. Only the Lord sees and hears and speaks, for the gods of the pagan world are man-made objects of wood and stone and silicon and plastic.

17. The kings of Assyria have laid waste: In his prayer of urgent supplication, Hezekiah did not gloss over the truth of his situation; neither did he attempt any false piety. He told the Lord frankly that the enemy spoke the truth in their claims of crushing other nations and destroying their false gods. Yet in the process he did not lose sight of the truth of God's character, and he did not give in to the fear, as the Assyrians hoped. He reminded himself that the enemy triumphed over other nations because their gods were not gods at all, while Judah was protected by the Creator of the universe.

19. THAT ALL THE KINGDOMS OF THE EARTH MAY KNOW: Hezekiah understood the Lord's larger purposes in His dealings with the nations. He protected the children of Israel because He had promised to do so, but His overall intention was that the world around Israel and Judah would come to a saving knowledge of Himself by seeing His faithfulness to them. The Lord is pleased when His people take His glory seriously.

GOD'S RESPONSE: *The Lord hears Hezekiah's prayer and intervenes for His people. His glory will be shown throughout the earth.*

20. BECAUSE YOU HAVE PRAYED TO ME: This is an important clause. It implies that the Lord delivered Judah from the hands of the Assyrians because they turned to Him for help. Israel, by contrast, had refused to humble themselves before the Lord, and they were taken into captivity by these same Assyrians.

22. WHOM HAVE YOU REPROACHED AND BLASPHEMED: The Lord took the Assyrians' words personally, even though much of their mockery was directed against Judah. The Lord identifies Himself with His people; what is done to His children is done to Him.

25. I HAVE BROUGHT IT TO PASS: Sennacherib thought that he had accomplished his military victories by his own power and majesty, but the Lord laughed him to scorn. Those victories occurred only because they were part of God's plan, and the Lord merely used the Assyrians as a man might use a weapon. Sennacherib could not boast of conquering cities any more than a sword can boast of slaying foes—it is the One who wields the weapon who gets the glory.

↣ FIRST IMPRESSIONS ↢

1. *If you had been standing on the walls of Judah, listening to the Assyrian's words, how would you have responded? Why did Hezekiah command the people to remain silent?*

2.   What were the basic threats and accusations leveled by the Assyrian messenger? What truth was there in his words? What lies?

3.   What was the Assyrian's goal in shouting his challenges at the people of Judah? How does the world attempt to do the same to Christians today?

4.   What aspects of God's character did Hezekiah focus on in his prayers? How might his prayers be a model for your prayers when faced with difficult circumstances?

ᨒ Some Key Principles ᨒ

Do not be drawn into debate with sin.

King Sennacherib's spokesman stood outside the walls of Judah, lying and blaspheming for all to hear. He accused Hezekiah of tearing down the Lord's sacred altars; he mocked the army of Judah; he claimed that Sennacherib was bringing the fulfillment of God's judgment on His people; he defied the Lord and denied the power of Judah's God. And all the while, the people of Judah were crowded atop the city walls, listening to the intimidation and taunts of the Assyrians, hearing them blaspheme the Lord, enduring the threats of starvation and captivity—and answering not a word.

King Hezekiah demonstrated wisdom when he commanded the people to remain silent. He did not want anyone to enter into debate with the enemy, for such debate leads only to further debate and eventually into despair or sin. Eve quite literally met the devil in the garden of Eden, and he lured her into a sort of debate concerning the meaning of God's command. She stood and talked with him, and the conversation concluded when she reached out and sinned against God. The people of Judah were facing a human being rather than Satan, but the same principle applied. The Assyrian was speaking the lies of the devil, and God's people were wise to remain silent.

The Lord Jesus demonstrated the best approach when confronted with the lies of the enemy when He was fasting in the wilderness at the beginning of His earthly ministry. When the devil came and tempted Him, the Lord's answer was to quote Scripture and command the enemy, "Get behind Me, Satan!" (Luke 4:8). There was no debate, no interaction concerning the "deeper meanings" of the Scriptures; the Lord simply meditated upon God's Word while commanding the devil to depart. This is the model for all believers to follow whenever we find ourselves confronted by the lies of the evil one: meditate on the Word of God, and call upon the Lord to drive away the enemy of our souls.

Christians must know how to rightly divide God's Word.

The Assyrians besieged the people of Judah with a war of words, using twisted logic, false statements, and terrible threats to break their spirit and cast them into fear. What made it worse was that much of what they said sounded plausible. They pointed to their many past victories over cities that were stronger than Judah, and they laid out in detail what their plans were for starving them into submission. The propaganda reached its most dangerous level, however, when the Assyrians reminded the people of the words spoken by their own prophet Isaiah, effectively quoting Scripture in an effort to convince them of their lies.

This principle is closely related to the previous one, for the devil loves to misuse God's Word to lead Christians astray. He used that tactic on Eve when he misquoted the Lord's command (Genesis 3:1), and he even tried to misapply Scripture with Jesus, quoting verses to support sin (Luke 4:9–11). But the Lord knew how to handle the Scriptures correctly, and His response to the devil's misapplied quotation was to counter with a more pertinent passage.

Paul addressed these important topics in a letter to Timothy. He warned Timothy to guard his flock against the dangers of idle debate, "charging them before the Lord not to strive about words to no profit, to the ruin of the hearers," training them instead to become deeply rooted in the Word of God. "Be diligent to present yourself approved to God," wrote Paul, "a worker who does not need to be ashamed, rightly dividing the word of truth. But shun profane and idle babblings, for they will increase to more ungodliness" (2 Timothy 2:14–16). We learn to rightly divide God's Word by studying it, memorizing it, and asking God for wisdom in applying it. In so doing, we arm ourselves against the attacks of the evil one.

God hears prayer.

Hezekiah was overwhelmed with the threat facing his people. Assyria was the most powerful nation on earth, and the cruelty of her army was renowned. Many other cities had fallen before their might and been carried away into captivity—and that included Judah's sister, Israel. The recent defeat and captivity of Judah's fellow Jews was undoubtedly fresh in Hezekiah's mind, as he had seen the Lord permit His people to be defeated by the Assyrians because of their idolatry, and he knew that Judah had committed the same sins. Now that same enemy was literally at his gates, openly declaring their intentions of destroying the city.

But Hezekiah did not give in to the fear that gripped him. Instead, he went into the house of God and spread before Him the defiant letter from Sennacherib, pouring out his heavy heart and asking the Lord to intervene. And this was just what the Lord wanted; He was pleased that His servant came to Him with his troubles instead of attempting to resolve them on his own. What's more, Hezekiah had taken an unbearable burden, a weight that he was not strong enough to carry, and he had given it to the Lord to carry. He probably felt as though he was walking on air when he rose up from prayer that day.

In order to lay our burdens before God, however, we must first humble ourselves to the point of recognizing that we are not strong enough to carry them. Hezekiah humbled himself, and the Lord picked up the burden. The Lord wants to bear our burdens for us, but He also wants us to ask for His help. It is pride that hinders our asking. "Be clothed with humility," Peter wrote to the church, for "'God resists the proud, but gives grace to the humble.' Therefore humble yourselves under the mighty hand of God, that He may exalt you in due time, casting all your care upon Him, for He cares for you" (1 Peter 5:5–7).

⌖ Digging Deeper ⌖

5. *Why did God allow Israel to be taken into captivity by Assyria? Why did He not allow the same fate for Judah?*

6. *In what ways does the world today try to engage Christians in futile debates? What should a Christian's response be to such debates?*

7. *What does it mean to rightly divide the word of truth? How is this done? Why is it important?*

8. What does it mean to spread your troubles before the Lord? How can you do that? What troubles do you need to spread at His feet this week?

↬ Taking It Personally ↫

9. How diligent are you at present in understanding and applying God's Word? What will you do this week to grow stronger in this area?

10. Are you jealous to guard the Lord's glory, as revealed through your life to others? Are there areas in your life that might be causing others to doubt His Word?

Section 3:

Themes

In This Section:

~ 10 ~
RENEWING GOD'S WORD

↳ THEMATIC BACKGROUND ↰

This study occurs during the reign of King Josiah, whose rule came near the end of Judah's history. Josiah was a very good king. He walked faithfully in obedience to God's Word throughout his life, and he was very zealous to obey God in all things. Unlike other godly kings, Josiah removed the high places and utterly destroyed all remnants of pagan worship throughout both Judah and Israel. So it might seem surprising that the Lord's judgment fell so swiftly on His people after the reign of such a godly man.

The reason is that the people's hearts had become hardened toward God, and after Josiah's death, Judah returned to paganism. The same pattern had occurred repeatedly throughout Judah's history: a godly king would arise and turn the people back to the Lord; then an ungodly man would follow and turn them back to paganism. Nevertheless, the Lord continued to show mercy and grace to Judah, and He restored to them the Book of the Law that had been lost. In this study, we will see Judah's last godly king lead the nation back to the Lord for one final period of faithfulness. His example can help us avoid Judah's rebellious pattern.

↳ READING 2 CHRONICLES 34:14–33 ↰

THE LOST BOOK: *King Josiah commands the repair to the temple in Jerusalem, and an interesting discovery is made.*

14. THE MONEY THAT WAS BROUGHT INTO THE HOUSE OF THE LORD: The temple had been repaired and refurbished under Joash, as we saw in Study 8, but it had once again fallen into disrepair. (These events occurred roughly two hundred years after Joash restored the temple.) The neglect of God's temple coincided with the syncretism of the people. The more they added pagan elements to their worship, the less they frequented the temple in Jerusalem—which was the only place where the Lord wanted them to worship.

THE BOOK OF THE LAW: This was probably a scroll containing a portion of Deuteronomy. The fact that it was discovered indicates that it had been long forgotten, a tragic implication of the unfaithfulness of God's people—the very people who had been entrusted with God's written revelation. The Lord reveals Himself to the world through His written Word and through the life of His Son Jesus, and He expects those who belong to Him to be faithful in making His character known to others. Misplacing and forgetting the Book of the Law was a terrible dereliction of duty on the part of the Jews.

16. ALL THAT WAS COMMITTED TO YOUR SERVANTS: That is, the people were carrying out the king's orders for the restoration of the temple.

CONFRONTED BY SIN: *The king reads the Book of the Law and is disconcerted by what he finds.*

19. HE TORE HIS CLOTHES: King Josiah was overcome with grief because he realized that God's people had completely forsaken His Law, and perhaps because he was shocked at his own ignorance of the sacred writings. Judah had been inventing their own religious methods and practices for so long that they no longer knew what was written in God's Word.

21. CONCERNING THE WORDS OF THE BOOK: Josiah was overwhelmed to discover his own lack of knowledge of the Law, realizing in the process how far away the people had drifted from following it. He asked some of his servants to go before the Lord and seek His wisdom on what they needed to do concerning the Book of the Law.

GREAT IS THE WRATH OF THE LORD: The Lord had repeatedly warned His people to not serve the gods of the pagans in Canaan, but to study and obey His Word instead. He had also commanded them to be diligent in teaching His Word to their children to ensure that His people would not forget His commands and go after false gods. If the people failed to keep His Word, He had promised to remove them from the land of Canaan. (See Deuteronomy 6.)

24. ALL THE CURSES THAT ARE WRITTEN IN THE BOOK: As we have seen in previous studies, the Lord always keeps His promises—both for blessings and for judgment.

25. MY WRATH WILL BE POURED OUT ON THIS PLACE: The Lord was not being hard-hearted toward Judah, for He had warned them repeatedly to stop adding pagan practices to their worship of Him. The time period covered in these studies alone is nearly 350 years, and we have seen how the Lord continually sent prophets to His people to turn them away from false gods and back to Himself—yet they persistently refused. And this is only the period after Solomon was king in Israel; the Lord had given these warnings to His people in the time of Moses, nearly five hundred years before the divided kingdom. As we have already noted, the time of judgment does eventually arrive if God's people continue to disobey His Word, and Judah had no excuse for their sins of paganism.

27. BECAUSE YOUR HEART WAS TENDER: A tender heart is the opposite of a hard heart. It is malleable, like soft clay, allowing the Lord to shape it and mold it until it is similar to His own. Josiah had not hardened his heart in stubbornness when he read the lost Book of the Law; instead, he had humbled himself and repented of his sins in grief and sorrow. This is exactly what the Lord wants His people to do when they are convicted of sin. As David wrote after committing a sin, "The sacrifices of God are a broken spirit, a broken and a contrite heart—these, O God, You will not despise" (Psalm 51:17).

PUBLIC READING OF GOD'S WORD: *The king reads the Book of the Law to the entire nation of Judah, and they make a covenant of obedience.*

30. HE READ IN THEIR HEARING: The Lord had commanded the kings of Israel (and Judah) to write their own copy of the Law by hand, and to read from it every day (Deuteronomy 17:18–20). He had also commanded the priests to read the whole Law to the entire nation at least once every seven years (Deuteronomy 31:10–13). It is possible that King Josiah discovered these commands in the fragment he read. It truly was a great tragedy that the priests of Judah did not possess a complete copy of the Law; all they had was this fragment, so even this public reading was incomplete.

31. MADE A COVENANT: Josiah fulfilled God's intended role for the kings of Israel and Judah by leading His people into obedience. He led both by example and by command, first obeying the Lord's commands in his own life so that his people could have a role model to follow.

WITH ALL HIS HEART AND ALL HIS SOUL: That is, inside and out, with his entire being—body, spirit, and mind. This phrase also harks back to Deuteronomy, a passage known as the Shema: "Hear, O Israel: The LORD our God, the LORD is one! You shall love the LORD your God with all your heart, with all your soul, and with all your strength" (Deuteronomy 6:4–5).

33. JOSIAH REMOVED ALL THE ABOMINATIONS: This chapter of 2 Chronicles opens with a list of the things that Josiah did to cleanse the land of its abominable practices. Unlike most of the prior kings, he also removed the high places. And when Josiah removed an abomination, he did more than simply put it to one side—he burned it to ashes or ground it to powder.

Ꭶ FIRST IMPRESSIONS Ꭷ

1. *What made the Book of the Law so valuable? What might have led up to its being lost? How did its being misplaced likely affect the people?*

2. *Why did King Josiah react so strongly upon reading the Book of the Law? What were his responsibilities? What were the priests' responsibilities?*

3. *Why did the Lord hold His people accountable to the Law, even though it had been lost? Why did He show them mercy at this time?*

4. *What does it mean to keep God's commandments with all one's heart and soul?*

↤ Some Key Principles ↦

God requires a love for His Word.

The Lord had given the people of Israel a sacred trust when He revealed Himself to them through His Law. The nation of Israel were the only people on earth who possessed such a collection of writings, God's Word spoken directly to His servant Moses, in which He taught the people how to live righteously before Him. The Lord's intention was that Israel would be an example to the nations around them, showing forth the grace and mercy of God to the Gentiles. To that end, the Lord commanded Israel to preserve His Word, to guard it jealously and to pass it on faithfully.

Instead, the people of Israel and Judah forsook God's Word and began imitating the polytheistic nations around them. The process began with adding elements from pagan religions into their worship of the Lord, but gradually those pagan elements took precedence over God's Word. By the time of Josiah, the people had disregarded His Word for so long that it had been all but forgotten—and some of their sacred writings were evidently lost. This would not have happened if the Lord's people had obeyed His commands to teach His Word to their children, as we considered in a previous study.

Christians today have the same responsibility to God's Word. The Bible contains God's written revelation about Himself, and it provides everything we need "for doctrine, for reproof, for correction, for instruction in righteousness, that the man of God may be complete, thoroughly equipped for every good work" (2 Timothy 3:16–17). But if we are to gain its blessings, we must maintain its regular use in our homes and churches. We must also be diligent to teach God's Word to the next generation, training younger men and women to read it, meditate on it, and apply it to their lives. The example of Israel in Josiah's day must stand as a warning to God's people: keep His Word central in all things, so that it will never again be lost.

Keep your heart tender toward God's Word.

The Lord commended King Josiah because his heart was tender, meaning that it was easily affected by a sense of his guilt before the Lord. When a wound is tender, it is very sensitive to the touch, and the slightest brushing will cause pain. This is the sense of the tender heart as well: a person with a tender heart is quick to recognize sin in his life, and that recognition causes pain and remorse. It is the opposite of a hard heart, which is insensitive to one's guilt and unresponsive to the Spirit's attempts to bring change.

Another metaphor is found in a lump of clay. A potter likes to work with clay that is soft and moldable, because only then can he fashion it into a vessel fit for a king. When clay becomes hard, it cannot be properly shaped, so the potter is forced to beat and knead the clay until it accepts moisture and becomes malleable once more. The human heart is prone to drying out and becoming hard like that lump of clay, forcing the Lord to use hardship and discipline to soften it up and make it fit for His hands.

The condition of our hearts is up to us. We harden or soften our hearts according to how we respond to God's Word: ignoring its teachings leads to a hard heart that becomes unresponsive to the Holy Spirit, while faithful obedience keeps it soft and malleable. The writer of Hebrews warns us, "Beware, brethren, lest there be in any of you an evil heart of unbelief in departing from the living God; but exhort one another daily, while it is called 'Today,' lest any of you be hardened through the deceitfulness of sin. For we have become partakers of Christ if we hold the beginning of our confidence steadfast to the end, while it is said: 'Today, if you will hear His voice, do not harden your hearts as in the rebellion'" (Hebrews 3:12–15).

Scripture calls people to repent and obey without delay.

King Josiah had been living in obedience to the Lord's commands, as far as he understood them. He had walked in the ways of King David, following the path of righteousness; "he did not turn aside to the right hand or to the left" (2 Chronicles 34:2). But one day, unexpectedly, he was handed God's Word to read—and he discovered that the nation of Judah had been walking in disobedience for generations. Yet his response was exactly what the Lord desired. He did not try to justify his people's sins by claiming that they didn't have the written Law earlier; instead, he humbled himself before the Lord and acknowledged that he and his nation had fallen far short of His commands.

This principle goes hand in hand with the previous one, since it is the method by which a believer keeps his heart soft. There are times for all believers when the Lord draws our attention to an area of sin in our lives through His Word and His Spirit. He does this because He wants His children to grow into the image and likeness of Christ, which entails an ongoing process of purification. The Word of God functions with the indwelling help of His Spirit to show us areas that need to be brought into conformance with His image, and our part is to comply with His Spirit's promptings. The Lord wants His children to be responsive in this process, just as King Josiah was, and quick to address the areas He brings to our attention.

King David set an excellent example of this process. He had committed grievous sins of adultery and murder, and he had tried to continue on with his life as though he had done nothing wrong. But the Lord confronted him through His prophet Nathan, and David immediately confessed his sin and repented before the Lord (2 Samuel 12). King Joash, in contrast, set the opposite example, as we saw in a previous study. When he was confronted by the Lord's prophet, he became angry and hardened his heart, and his refusal to repent led him into even more grievous sins. John reminded his readers, "If we confess our sins, He is faithful and just to forgive us our sins and to cleanse us from all unrighteousness. If we say that we have not sinned, we make Him a liar, and His word is not in us" (1 John 1:9–10).

⤳ DIGGING DEEPER ⤲

5. In your own words, what does it mean to have a tender heart? How does one keep his or her heart tender? Why is it important?

6. How does God's Word become lost? What leads to this tragedy? How is it avoided?

7. Why is immediate repentance important? What leads a person to being convicted of sin? How is repentance accomplished?

8. When has God's Word convicted you of an area of disobedience of which you'd been previously unaware? How did you respond?

↜ Taking It Personally ↝

9. What are you doing at present to keep God's Word from being lost or forgotten? What are you doing to train the next generation?

10. Compared to a lump of clay, what state is your heart in currently? Soft and malleable? Hard as a rock? Somewhere in between? What will you do this week to make it softer?

BEING WHOLEHEARTED FOR GOD

2 CHRONICLES 15

⟿ THEMATIC BACKGROUND ⟿

Throughout these studies, we have met men and women who were wholehearted in their devotion to God, and others who were not. We have seen quite clearly that wholeheartedness often leads to blessing and reward, while halfheartedness often leads to destruction. But what exactly does it mean to be wholehearted for God? What role do our faith and our actions play?

In Study 3, we met King Asa, a man who was wholehearted in his service to the Lord. When we left him at the end of that study, he had led the army of Judah in a miraculous victory over the Ethiopian army. You will remember that the Ethiopians were vastly superior to Judah, both in numbers and in equipment. Judah's army consisted of 280,000 foot soldiers, while the Ethiopian army had more than a million men and hundreds of chariots. (See 2 Chronicles 14 for details.) In this study, we will rejoin King Asa as he returns to Judah.

A man named Azariah, sent by the Lord with a word of encouragement, met the king. Though Asa had been a part of a miraculous victory from God, the Lord knew that Asa was in need of an encouraging reminder of God's ever-present involvement with His people. Azariah reminded Asa that if we obey God, He will bless us. If we are not faithful to God, He will discipline us. In this study, we will see that all of God's people need such encouragement, because of its important role in remaining wholehearted for the Lord.

⟿ READING 2 CHRONICLES 15:1–19 ⟿

A WORD OF ENCOURAGEMENT: *King Asa returns from battle (see Study 3) and is met by Azariah with a word of encouragement from God.*

1. AZARIAH: Nothing further is known of this man, but his appearance here demonstrates that the Lord had many in Israel and Judah who were still faithful to His Word during these days of apostasy.

2. WHILE YOU ARE WITH HIM: The Lord made similar promises to many of the kings of Israel and Judah, including Solomon, and it was conditional: if the king would walk in faithfulness to God's commands, He would bless both king and nation—but only if the king walked in obedience, as David did. Asa did so, for the most part, and the Lord blessed his reign.

IF YOU SEEK HIM: This is a basic principle of the Christian life: the Lord wants His people to seek Him. Christianity is not a passive relationship with God; it is active, and the believer's role is to be constantly seeking Him.

SEEK GOD: *The Lord commands Asa to seek Him with his whole heart—and He promises that He will be found.*

---

3. ISRAEL HAS BEEN WITHOUT THE TRUE GOD: This does not mean that the Lord had abandoned His people, but the opposite: the people of Israel and Judah had abandoned the worship practices that God had ordained and had consequently moved away from Him.

WITHOUT A TEACHING PRIEST: This statement reveals a significant part of the problem that God's people faced: the priests had gradually stopped teaching them. Part of the priestly function was to "distinguish between holy and unholy, and between unclean and clean," and to "teach the children of Israel all the statutes which the LORD has spoken to them" (Leviticus 10:10–11). When God's priests abandon their responsibilities, the people are sure to follow.

WITHOUT LAW: This naturally follows when the priesthood stops teaching: the people forget God's Word. We saw the long-term results of this trend in our last study, where the people of Judah had quite literally lost the written Law of God. In most of our studies in this book, we have concentrated on the king's role in leading the people either toward God or away from Him, but here we are reminded that the priests also had responsibility for the spiritual condition of their nation.

4. HE WAS FOUND BY THEM: This is an important principle to understand: the Lord *wants* to be found by men—but men must *seek* Him. The process of seeking God is not a mystical search for hidden knowledge; neither is it an end in itself. One seeks God through prayer and study of His Word. He has revealed His character in the Scriptures, and He reveals His will through Scripture, prayer, and the Holy Spirit. People today often speak of the "spiritual journey" as though the journey itself were the goal, but the journeying and seeking are merely how we *reach* the goal, which is to know God and to become like Him.

5. NO PEACE . . . BUT GREAT TURMOIL: This is the natural lifestyle for the person who does not know God. Without Christ, all men are spiritually blind; and like the blind, they stumble about without understanding, tripping over things that they cannot even correctly identify. People who deny God will try to find satisfaction and meaning in their lives through pleasure or wealth or power or occult practices or just about any new fad that comes along, but all those false methods lead only to turmoil and destruction.

6. GOD TROUBLED THEM WITH EVERY ADVERSITY: The Lord sends trouble into the people's lives for the same reason He sends blessings: to move them toward Himself, not because He gains some sadistic pleasure in seeing His creatures suffer. He simply desires that we would be in intimate relationship with Him.

BE STRONG: *The Lord commands Asa to be strong and courageous.*

7. BE STRONG: Notice that the Lord's command here is to *be* strong, not to *become* strong. There is a distinct element of volition, the idea that we are strong because we choose to be—that we choose to not allow our hands to be weak. This volition refers to our determination to be wholehearted for God, rather than halfhearted, as were so many of the kings we've been studying. It means to obey God's Word in all areas of our lives, outwardly and inwardly, in all settings and situations. It means to set our hearts on knowing Him and not allowing anything to hinder us in that process.

YOUR WORK SHALL BE REWARDED: The work referred to here is the effort involved in seeking God with a whole heart, refusing to allow any other forces to take a higher priority in his life. Asa's reward would be godliness and wisdom, because God is faithful to reveal Himself to those who seek.

8. HE TOOK COURAGE: It is also interesting to note the role played by Azariah in this process. He helped the king recover his courage by speaking words of encouragement, reminding him that the Lord always rewards those who faithfully seek Him.

REMOVED THE ABOMINABLE IDOLS: Here again we see the importance of encouraging words. The king had not removed the false idols from the land as yet, but he found the courage to obey God completely when Azariah reminded him of God's faithfulness.

9. WHEN THEY SAW THAT THE LORD HIS GOD WAS WITH HIM: One man's courageous obedience to God's commands led others to be courageous as well. "As iron sharpens iron, so a man sharpens the countenance of his friend" (Proverbs 27:17); likewise, the wholehearted obedience of one man deepens the commitment of others.

12. WITH ALL THEIR HEART AND WITH ALL THEIR SOUL: We encountered this phrase in our last study, and it is the key to being wholehearted for God. It means to make Him the absolute highest priority in every aspect of our lives, beginning with our thought lives and extending outward to our actions and attitudes.

13. PUT TO DEATH: Christians today are not called to put unbelievers to death, yet this extreme action on the king's part does underscore the importance of maintaining godly relationships. Believers are commanded to share the gospel with unbelievers today, just as God wanted Israel to share His glory with the nations around them. But within the nation of Israel, as within God's body today, His people are called to hold one another to high standards of obedience to His Word.

14. WITH SHOUTING AND TRUMPETS AND RAMS' HORNS: It is a cause of celebration when a man or woman commits to following God with a whole heart. The very angels in heaven rejoice when a soul repents (Luke 15:10).

⌁ FIRST IMPRESSIONS ⌁

1. *Asa was returning from a miraculous victory over the Ethiopian army. Why did God send him a word of encouragement at that point? What role did the encouragement serve after his victory?*

2. *In your own words, what does it mean to seek God? Why does He want us to seek Him? How is this done?*

3. *Why are God's people so frequently commanded to be strong and without fear? Why is this so critical? What is true about God's character that makes obedience to this command possible?*

4. *How did Asa's courage influence others? What part did Azariah play in this? What part did Asa's own volition play?*

↶ Some Key Principles ↷

Seek the Lord, and He will be found.

Throughout these studies, we have encountered the theme of seeking God. Some of the kings of Judah sought God, while many did not; but in both cases, the seeker found what he was seeking. King Asa sought the Lord, and he found Him; King Rehoboam sought idols, and he found them. The end result of each choice is self-evident: seeking the Lord leads to life; seeking idols leads to death. One wonders why anyone would ever choose to *not* seek God.

Many Christians try to coast through life taking the "laid-back," easy route. They believe that by not actively seeking false gods, they are actively seeking God. But that is not the case; seeking God is more than not seeking idols. It is an active pursuit, something that believers must deliberately choose to do. This is done by studying God's Word on a regular basis; by meeting with other believers regularly for worship, Bible study, and prayer; and by regular times of prayer and confession privately before the Lord. It also requires that we be on guard at all times to ensure that nothing else in life ever takes a higher priority than the pursuit of God. If we choose to not make this deliberate choice, we are effectively choosing to not seek God.

The good news is that the process of seeking God is not burdensome or difficult. Indeed, the Lord is busier seeking us than we could ever be seeking Him, and He so vehemently wants us to find Him that He was willing to sacrifice His Son on the cross to make it possible. All that is required of us is to humble ourselves before Him, confess our sins, and submit to His lordship in all areas of our lives. When we do this, He has promised that He will be found. "Draw near to God and He will draw near to you. Cleanse your hands, you sinners; and purify your hearts, you double-minded. . . . Humble yourselves in the sight of the Lord, and He will lift you up" (James 4:8, 10).

Take courage from the encouragement of God's Word.

It seems an odd moment for God to send a prophet with words of encouragement to King Asa. He had just returned from a miraculous victory over the seemingly superior Ethiopians. Asa was a godly king, giving due credit to God for the victory. He walked in the ways of David and sought to obey God in his life. And yet, God chose to encourage King Asa with the reminder of who He was and what He expected of His people. Interestingly, 2 Chronicles tells us that Asa "took courage" when he heard Azariah's words (v. 8). This courage enabled him to take strong action against the abominable idols that were scattered throughout the land. The story of Asa's life does not show any hint of cowardice, yet evidently the Lord knew that he needed to have his courage bolstered in that moment to enable him to take that extra step of obedience.

We have noticed repeatedly throughout these studies that the Lord commands His people to stand strong against fear and despair. This story of Asa reveals another way to obey that command. We will find encouragement by reading and studying God's Word, and we can also serve as a vehicle of that encouragement by sharing with others what we learn. A study of God's Word will reveal that God is both sovereign and faithful. He is in control of every event in our lives, and He is faithfully at work molding each of His children into the image of Christ. Isaiah wrote, "Strengthen the weak hands, and make firm the feeble knees. Say to those who are fearful-hearted, 'Be strong, do not fear! Behold, your God will come with vengeance, with the recompense of God; He will come and save you.' Then the eyes of the blind shall be opened, and the ears of the deaf shall be unstopped. Then the lame shall leap like a deer, and the tongue of the dumb sing" (Isaiah 35:3–6).

Love God wholeheartedly.

Over and over in these studies, we have encountered the admonition to love God with all our hearts. What exactly does this mean? To love God with all our hearts means that we are to love God with every aspect of our being, including our thoughts and affections. The heart is the part of us that thinks and wills and makes determinations, the seat of our conscious volition.

In a theological sense, our obedience to God begins with God Himself, for it is only through His power and intervention in our lives that we are able to obey Him in any respect. But from a human perspective, our obedience and commitment to God's Word begins with our hearts, with our minds and volition—and particularly with our thoughts. This is the reason we are commanded to guard our hearts, as Solomon warned when he wrote, "Keep your heart with all diligence, for out of it spring the issues of life"

(Proverbs 4:23). We become wholehearted for God by first deciding in our hearts and minds that it is our top priority.

Our thinking determines who we become. The natural man or woman wants to think about fleshly pursuits, and this leads a person to become conformed to the image of the world. Christians are called to transform their minds, to change from fleshly thinking to godly thinking—and this is the first step in becoming wholehearted for God. Paul wrote, "I beseech you therefore, brethren, by the mercies of God, that you present your bodies a living sacrifice, holy, acceptable to God, which is your reasonable service. And do not be conformed to this world, but be transformed by the renewing of your mind, that you may prove what is that good and acceptable and perfect will of God" (Romans 12:1–2).

∽ Digging Deeper ∽

5. *In your own words, what does it mean to be wholehearted for God? What part do you play? What part does the Holy Spirit play?*

6. *What does it mean to renew your mind? How is this done? Why is it important?*

7. *Who benefits from encouragement? Why is it such a basic part of healthy Christian fellowship?*

8. When has someone helped you with a timely word of encouragement? What specifically encouraged you in that situation? How can this help you to encourage others?

↜ TAKING IT PERSONALLY ↝

9. Do you tend to be encouraging or discouraging to others? How can you be an encouragement this week to those around you?

10. Do you seek God wholeheartedly? What needs to change in order to say yes? Do you have a plan in place that will help you to consistently study God's Word, pray, and be with others in Christian fellowship?

SECTION 4:

SUMMARY

NOTES AND PRAYER REQUESTS

REVIEWING KEY PRINCIPLES

∽ LOOKING BACK ∽

Over the course of the preceding eleven studies, we have witnessed a repetitive cycle in Judah of godly kings followed by ungodly kings, leaders who strove to obey God's commands followed by those who wanted to lead the nation into paganism. As time went along, the people of Judah became more and more hardened in their pagan practices, and the spiritual revivals lasted for shorter and shorter periods of time. Yet through it all, the Lord remained faithful to His people, always sending godly men and women who spoke boldly for His Word.

Eventually, however, God's patience came to an end, and the nation of Judah went into captivity, just as Israel had done previously. Yet even in this, the Lord was faithful to His people and to His promises, and after their seventy years in captivity, He began to bring His people back to Jerusalem. The one thing that remains constant throughout these studies is this: God is always faithful, even when His people are not.

Here are a few of the major principles we have found in this book. There are many more that we don't have room to reiterate, so take some time to review the earlier studies—or better still, to meditate upon the passages of Scripture that we have covered. Ask the Holy Spirit to give you wisdom and insight into His Word. He will not refuse.

∽ SOME KEY PRINCIPLES ∽

God's people are called to be hospitable.

The woman in this story set an excellent example of hospitality. She knew that Elisha, the Lord's servant, was making regular trips throughout the northern tribes of Israel, tracing a route that took him past her home periodically. She saw a need and met it by providing Elisha with a home away from home. This provision was costly to her and her husband, both financially and personally. They remodeled their home at financial cost to themselves, and they opened up their lives by sharing meals with God's servant.

The book of Hebrews reminds us that we, too, are to share with complete strangers: "Do not forget to entertain strangers, for by so doing some have unwittingly entertained angels" (13:2). Genesis 18 recounts a time when Abraham entertained angels—and even the Lord Himself in a preincarnate appearance. Three strangers arrived at Abraham's camp, and he leaped up to welcome them and to prepare a sumptuous meal for them, little knowing at the time whom he was entertaining. He was tremendously blessed for his hospitality, as the Lord shared His plans for the coming judgment on Sodom and Gomorrah. If Abraham had not been hospitable, he might have missed that blessing.

Jesus taught His disciples that when they showed hospitality to others, they were effectively showing it to Him (Matthew 25:34–40). Peter further instructed his readers, "Be hospitable to one another without grumbling" (1 Peter 4:9). The Shunammite woman provided hospitality without begrudging the cost, and the Lord used this warmth to bless and strengthen His servant Elisha. He also blessed the Shunammite couple, giving them a son in their old age, and miraculously raising him from the dead. Hospitality is a gift that blesses twice, giving to the giver as well as the receiver.

God is in control of life and death.

Elisha faced the timeless dilemma: what to get the woman who had everything. Unlike the widow who was on the verge of starvation, this Shunammite woman had wealth and a husband. But she was barren, and it seems she had given up hope of having a child. Elisha knew that only God can give life, and thus if she received a baby it would be obvious that it was a gift from the Lord.

But when the child died, the Shunammite woman knew this, too, was from the Lord. She did not blame her husband, sickness, or any other factor for the boy's death. Instead she went straight to the man of God. Likewise, Elisha knew the child's death was from the Lord. In fact, it was obvious that no power inherent in Elisha raised the boy to life, rather, it was God who answered Elisha's fervent prayer. Just as the boy's death was from the Lord, so, too, was his new life.

Job, many centuries earlier, lost his children to untimely deaths. When his family was killed by demonically inspired but divinely permitted marauders, Job declared, "The LORD gave, and the LORD has taken away" (Job 1:21). Later he asked his wife, "Shall we indeed accept good from God, and shall we not also accept adversity?" (Job 2:10). Job understood the truth: that all of life is under the control of God. For this reason, we can have confidence in the face of death, but we can also rejoice that our God is the Author of life.

Christians must strive to finish the race well.

King Asa started out strong. He had a heart for God, and strove to obey His commands. He tore down the pagan altars in Judah and purified his own life from the idolatry of his forebears. He trusted fully in the Lord, even when circumstances seemed overwhelming. Unfortunately, he did not finish his reign as he had begun. By the end of his life, he had turned his heart away from trusting the Lord, preferring to place his faith in the wisdom and power of men.

King Solomon followed the same pattern, beginning his reign as a young man who called out to God for wisdom. But as time went along, Solomon's heart was turned away from obedience and toward paganism and idolatry. In both cases, the kings did not persevere in maintaining godliness and purity, and the result was tragic. Nothing is quite as sad as watching a man begin his life strong in his commitment to God, only to sink into worldliness and sin as time goes along.

Paul recognized this tendency in human nature to lose one's focus, and he strove to maintain a strong discipline over the flesh, guarding against those snares and temptations that can gradually lure a person away from God's Word. Comparing the Christian life to a marathon, he wrote: "Do you not know that those who run in a race all run, but one receives the prize? Run in such a way that you may obtain it. And everyone who competes for the prize is temperate in all things. Now they do it to obtain a perishable crown, but we for an imperishable crown. Therefore I run thus: not with uncertainty. Thus I fight: not as one who beats the air. But I discipline my body and bring it into subjection, lest, when I have preached to others, I myself should become disqualified" (1 Corinthians 9:24–27). The wise Christian will always remember to continue in spiritual training, staying the course for the long haul and striving to finish well.

The battle belongs to God—but we also have a role to play.

Jehoshaphat recognized that his people were powerless to defeat the terrible foe that came to destroy them, and he turned to the Lord. This was exactly the right response, for the Lord wants His people to let Him fight their battles, and God promised the king that He would rout the foe—"for the battle is not yours," said Jahaziel, "but God's" (2 Chronicles 20:15).

Nevertheless, this promise did not give the people of Judah the right to go home and take a nap until the war was over. The Lord was indeed going to do the fighting for them, but they still had a part to play in the conflict. It was not an aggressive part; on the contrary, their role was to take a position, stand firm in it, and watch. Their position was to trust that the Lord would keep His promises, then to stand firm in that faith even though they were faced with an overwhelming foe that threatened to destroy them. By standing firm in their faith, they were free to watch for God's great deliverance—and when it came, they saw that their faith was not in vain.

This is what it means to stand strong in the faith. We have the steadfast assurance that God will always keep His promises, and we can fully depend on Him to protect us and fight on our behalf against the enemy who seeks to destroy us. When we are firm in our faith, we can see God work in our lives for His glory, and we can also realize that all of the glory belongs to God. He will deliver us, and we will surely see that our faith is not in vain.

Occult activities are an attempt to replace God.

The idolatry of Israel and Judah began as syncretism, a blending of pagan ideas with the true worship of God—but it ended with the most hideous abominations, including child sacrifice. This was a clear testimony that the Israelites thought their own God was insufficient to guide them. They thought they needed protection and direction from other gods. While child sacrifice may sound like an extreme case, the fact is that all disobedience to God's Word eventually leads to abominable practices if the person does not repent and turn away from disobedience. By definition, sin is the act of choosing to follow inner desires rather than submitting to God, and all sin leads inexorably away from the Lord and toward evil.

Interestingly, the Lord includes child sacrifice in the category of occult abominations. Today this is practiced through the widespread sin of abortion. It is no coincidence that as Western civilization hardens its heart against God, sins like this are becoming more accepted.

Christians, of course, must have no part in such sins. God strictly forbade His people to even associate with "anyone who makes his son or his daughter pass through the fire, or one who practices witchcraft, or a soothsayer, or one who interprets omens, or a sorcerer, or one who conjures spells, or a medium, or a spiritist, or one who calls up the dead. For all who do these things are an abomination to the LORD, and because of these abominations the LORD your God drives them out from before you" (Deuteronomy 18:10–12). As Christians, our direction and protection is found in the Lord, and not through other means, such as the sacrifice of children.

The Lord will one day return to take His children home.

Elijah was one of only two men in the Bible who were taken to heaven without dying. His dramatic ascension in a whirlwind, accompanied by a chariot of fire and horses, demonstrated that God has absolute command over all the forces of nature, including death. It seemed utterly impossible to those left behind that a man might escape death, and the Scriptures tell us clearly that "it is appointed for men to die once" (Hebrews 9:27)—yet they searched diligently and found no body of Elijah, for there was none to find.

We are not told why God chose to do this for Elijah, yet part of His reason was to present a clear demonstration to His people that He is able to whisk them into His presence suddenly, in the twinkling of an eye. The Bible promises that this very thing will happen one day, when "the Lord Himself will descend from heaven with a shout, with the voice of an archangel, and with the trumpet of God. . . . Then we who are alive and remain shall be caught up . . . in the clouds to meet the Lord in the air. And thus we shall always be with the Lord" (1 Thessalonians 4:16–17).

Just as Elijah and Elisha lived as messengers of God and walked in faithfulness to Him, the apostle Paul stated that he would be rewarded with a crown of righteousness from the Lord. What's more, Paul said this crown will also be awarded to "all who have loved His appearing" (2 Timothy 4:8). For the person who walks in faithfulness to Jesus Christ, His return to earth to be with His people forever is a sight to be longed for and desired. Skeptics may doubt that the Lord can take someone from the earth miraculously and without experiencing death. But Elijah's departure is an encouragement for us to long for the Lord's coming.

Avoid the sin of ingratitude.

King Joash owed a great deal to the spiritual leadership and friendship of Jehoiada—indeed, he owed his very life to the high priest and his wife. Their act of preserving him from his grandmother's deadly plot was performed at great risk to themselves, for Athaliah would not have hesitated to kill them if she had caught them. Yet Jehoiada's gifts did not end with the preservation of Joash's life; the high priest undoubtedly taught the young boy from the Word of God during the years when he was living at the temple. He later gathered the people together and made Joash king, again at great risk to himself, and then continued to counsel him in the ways of righteousness.

But Joash forgot all these things; he "did not remember the kindness which Jehoiada his father had done to him" (2 Chronicles 24:22), and that same forgetfulness led him directly into a very great sin. How could a man forget such costly and selfless love, especially when he owed his kingship and his life to the man who'd been like a father to him? The answer to that question is found in the heart of every human being. We are all prone to commit the sin of ingratitude, just as we are prone to disobey God's commands. Joash fell into ingratitude because he forgot to remember the goodness God had shown to him through the life of Jehoida. When we fail to remember the goodness of God toward us, the result threatens us all.

Gratitude requires a person to remember the blessings he has received through the efforts of another, and that remembering requires deliberate effort. This is the reason that the Scriptures command us to deliberately remember all the Lord has done on our behalf, for without such deliberate recollection, we will quickly take His love and kindness for granted and fall prey to the sin of ingratitude. "Bless the LORD, O my soul," wrote the great ancestor of Joash, King David, "and forget not all His benefits" (Psalm 103:2). This is done by choosing to rejoice rather than complain, by intentionally focusing on a spirit of thankfulness, and by taking our gratitude directly to God. Paul wrote, "Rejoice always, pray without ceasing, in everything give thanks; for this is the will of God in Christ Jesus for you" (1 Thessalonians 5:16–18).

↳ DIGGING DEEPER ↲

1. *What are some of the more important things you have learned from the Scriptures we have studied in this book?*

2. *Which of the concepts or principles have you found most encouraging? Which have been most challenging?*

3. What aspects of "walking with God" are you already doing in your life? Which areas need strengthening?

4. Which of the characters we've studied have you felt the most drawn to? How might you emulate that person in your own life?

↳ Taking It Personally ↰

5. Have you taken a definite stand for Jesus Christ? Have you accepted His free gift of salvation? If not, what is preventing you?

6. What areas of your personal life have been most convicted during this study? What exact things will you do to address these convictions? Be specific.

7. What have you learned about God's character during this study? How has this insight affected your worship or prayer life?

8. List below the specific things you want to see God do in your life in the coming month. List also the things you intend to change in your own life in that time. Return to this list in one month and hold yourself accountable to fulfill these things.

If you would like to continue in your study of the Old Testament, read the next title in this series, *God's Presence During Hardship*, or the previous title, *A House Divided*.